Mapping ICT access in South Africa

Kholadi Tlabela, Joan Roodt & Andrew Paterson
with Gina Weir-Smith

Published by HSRC Press
Private Bag X9182, Cape Town, 8000, South Africa
www.hsrcpress.ac.za

First published 2007

ISBN 978-0-7969-2182-6

© 2007 The Universal Service and Access Agency of South Africa

Cover design by Jacob Erasmus @ Compress
Production management Compress / www.compress.co.za

Distributed in Africa by Blue Weaver
Tel: +27 (0) 21 701 4477; Fax: +27 (0) 21 701 7302
www.oneworldbooks.com

Distributed in Europe and the United Kingdom by Eurospan Distribution Services (EDS)
Tel: +44 (0) 20 7240 0856; Fax: +44 (0) 20 7379 0609
www.eurospangroup.com/bookstore

Distributed in North America by Independent Publishers Group (IPG)
Call toll-free: (800) 888 4741; Fax: +1 (312) 337 5985
www.ipgbook.com

CONTENTS

Tables and figures   iv
Acknowledgements   vi
Acronyms   vii
Executive summary   ix

1   INTRODUCTION   1
1.1   The importance of access to information and communications technology in South Africa   1
1.2   Universal ICT access and service in South Africa since 1994   2
1.3   Indicators of ICT access   3

2   ACCESS TO TELEPHONIC COMMUNICATIONS   7
2.1   Fixed telephone lines   8
2.2   Cellular subscribers   11
2.3   Community Service Telephones   16

3   ACCESS TO COMPUTERS AND THE INTERNET   21
3.1   Access to computers   21
3.2   Access to the Internet   24

4   ACCESS TO INFORMATION AND TELECOMMUNICATIONS SERVICE CENTRES   29
4.1   Multi-Purpose Community Centres   30
4.2   Telecentres and Cyberlabs   36
4.3   Public Information Terminals   47
4.4   Libraries   49

5   UNDER-SERVICED AREAS   51
5.1   Under-Serviced Area Licences   51

6   COMPOSITE INDICATORS OF ACCESS TO ICT   53
6.1   Development of composite indicators   53
6.2   Composite indicator 1: Private access   53
6.3   Composite indicator 2: Public access   55

7   CONCLUSIONS AND RECOMMENDATIONS   58
7.1   Conclusions   58
7.2   Recommendations   59

APPENDICES   63
Appendix 1   63
Appendix 2   67
Appendix 3   68

REFERENCES   69

TABLES AND FIGURES

Tables

Table 2.1 Household access to landlines by province 9
Table 2.2 Household access to cellular phones by province 12
Table 2.3 Comparison of household access to telephone communications by province 13
Table 2.4 Provision of CSTs by cellular telephone service providers by province 16
Table 3.1 Percentage of household access to PCs by province 22
Table 3.2 Household access to the Internet by province 26
Table 4.1 Distribution of population within 5 km radius of MPCC by province 32
Table 4.2 Distribution of population within 5 km radius of MPCC by municipality 34
Table 4.3 Distribution of population within 5 km radius of a telecentre by province 37
Table 4.4 Distribution of population within a 5 km radius of a telecentre by municipality 39
Table 4.5 Distribution of secondary school aged population within a 5 km radius of a Cyberlab by province 42
Table 4.6 Distribution of secondary school aged population within a 5 km radius of a Cyberlab by municipality 43
Table 4.7: Distribution of population within a 5 km radius of a PIT by province 48
Table 4.8 Distribution of public libraries by province 50

Figures

Figure 2.1 Number of municipalities with percentage of households having landline access 10
Figure 2.2 Percentage of households with access to landlines per municipality 11
Figure 2.3 Number of municipalities with percentage of households having access to cellular phones 14
Figure 2.4 Household access to cellular phones per municipality 15
Figure 2.5 Number of municipalities by number of CSTs 17
Figure 2.6 Number of CSTs per municipality 18
Figure 2.7 Number of municipalities by number of CSTs per 1 000 people 18
Figure 2.8 Number of CSTs per 1 000 people per municipality 19
Figure 3.1 Number of municipalities with percentage of households having access to PCs 23
Figure 3.2 Household access to PCs per municipality 24
Figure 3.3 Number of municipalities with percentage of households having access to the Internet 27
Figure 3.4 Household access to the Internet per municipality 28

Figure 4.1	MPCCs showing serviced population within a 5 km radius 33
Figure 4.2	Number of MPCCs servicing estimated population numbers within a 5 km radius 33
Figure 4.3	Telecentres showing serviced population within a 5 km radius 38
Figure 4.4	Number of telecentres servicing estimated population numbers within a 5 km radius 38
Figure 4.5	Cyberlabs showing serviced secondary school aged population within a 5 km radius 43
Figure 4.6	Number of Cyberlabs showing secondary school aged population serviced within a 5 km radius 47
Figure 4.7	Number of PITs showing serviced population within a 5 km radius 49
Figure 5.1	Under-Serviced Area Licences per district municipality 52
Figure 6.1	Number of municipalities according to private access to ICT indicator 54
Figure 6.2	Indicator of private ICT access in South Africa per municipality 55
Figure 6.3	Number of municipalities according to public access to ICT indicator 56
Figure 6.4	Indicator of public access to ICT in South Africa per municipality 57
Figure A	Distribution of cellphone users per 1 000 people by municipality 64
Figure B	Cellphone users per 1 000 people 66

ACKNOWLEDGEMENTS

The authors would like to thank the following colleagues for their important contribution to the development of this publication:
- Colleagues from the Universal Service and Access Agency of South Africa who participated in project meetings, or as individuals contributed to the shape of this work;
- Sbo Zama for map creation and data management;
- Craig Schwabe for his advice as project leader;
- All colleagues from the Universal Service and Access Agency of South Africa and from the HSRC who engaged in the discussion about the indicators presented in this report; and
- Steve Esselaar of the LINK Centre, University of Johannesburg for his valuable comments and suggestions.

ACRONYMS

CITI	Cape Information Technology Initiative
CST	Community Service Telephones
GCIS	Government Communication and Information Service
GIS	Geographic Information System
ICASA	Independent Communications Authority of South Africa
ITU	International Telecommunications Union
MPCC	Multi-Purpose Community Centres
PC	personal computer
PITS	Public Information Terminals
SMME	small, medium and micro enterprises
USAASA	Universal Service and Access Agency of South Africa
USAL	under-serviced-area licences

EXECUTIVE SUMMARY

Background to the study

The current and future capacity of South Africa to generate and sustain access to information and communication technologies (ICTs) for its citizens is an important development priority. To achieve this development objective it is necessary to rollout ICT infrastructure on a national basis. This is an aim of government and, more specifically, of the Universal Service and Access Agency of South Africa (USAASA).

Information on the extent of ICT access and use in South Africa must feed planning to maximise the opportunities to exploit ICT for improved equity and social and economic development. There must be a clear understanding of what ICT access conditions currently exist (i.e. where we are now) and what gaps there are (i.e. what we need to do).

The USAASA commissioned the Human Sciences Research Council (HSRC) to conduct research to reveal spatial patterns of ICT access in South Africa. Available information tells us that ICT access – and usage – is distributed between different areas (e.g. rural-urban), and demographically between rich and poor, yet the spatial dimensions of this distribution have not been systematically analysed. This report seeks to explore this important issue by mapping access to ICT.

Methodology and indicators

Universal service is defined as 'the availability of a reliable connection to a communication network that enables any form of communication to and from any part of South Africa', while universal access refers to 'the ability to use a communication network at a reasonable distance and at an affordable price, which provides relevant information and has the necessary capacity' (USAASA 2004).

From this core formulation, the HSRC in consultation with the USAASA defined a set of indicators and data were obtained from relevant government data sources and from ICT service providers to populate the indicators. Where national census data for specific indicators were not available per individual or per household, it was necessary to model data obtained from national household survey datasets held by the HSRC. In the medium to long term it will be desirable to obtain the funding, create the infrastructure and develop methodological processes in order to promote sustainable statistical measures of ICT access in South Africa over time.

Based on the available datasets, 13 indicators were selected that most closely corresponded with indicators of ICT access applied internationally. When grouped the indicators refer to:
- access to telecommunications, computers and the Internet in the household;
- access to various forms of public telecommunications service centres; and
- access to telecommunications services in areas designated as under-serviced.

For each indicator, the raw data were integrated into a Geographic Information System (GIS) and then represented and analysed at the provincial and the municipal level. This provided the opportunity to compare differences in access to ICT across the provinces and across the 262 municipalities in South Africa.

Analysis

Eleven separate indicators of access to ICT and information were analysed in this report. The findings from selected indicators are provided below. Then, the high-level results from a composite indicator of private household access to ICT and a composite indicator of public provision of ICT are briefly reviewed.

Telecommunications

A key facet of personal and household communications is access to telecommunications. Nationally, the average level of household access to cellphones (33.1 per cent) is higher than the average access to landlines (23.6 per cent). However, the balance of access between landline and cellphones differs widely between provinces. The usage of cellphones compared to landlines is around 20 per cent higher in Gauteng and the North West, and 19 per cent higher in Limpopo. Both high cellphone and landline usage in Gauteng could possibly be attributed to a higher income level in the province than in other provinces. The high cellphone uptake in the North West and Limpopo could possibly be attributed to relatively low fixed-line availability in these provinces. Further analysis would be needed to establish the conditions that give rise to these patterns. However, the influence of a variety of factors – household income, availability of landlines, population density, market size – or a combination of these and other factors could be the probable cause.

Table: Comparison of household access to telephone communications by province

Province	Percentage households with cellphone	Percentage households with landline	Difference in percentage
Gauteng	48.7	28.5	20.2
Western Cape	46.7	55.3	-8.6
North West	35.3	15.0	20.3
KwaZulu-Natal	35.2	31.7	3.5
Free State	33.9	21.8	12.1
Mpumalanga	26.3	17.6	8.7
Limpopo	26.1	7.1	19.0
Eastern Cape	25.7	15.9	9.8
Northern Cape	20.1	20.0	0.1
National average	33.1	23.6	9.5

Source: Data from HSRC (2003)

Computers and the Internet

The findings are that 13.6 per cent of South African households could access a PC in 2003. Clearly, most citizens would not be able to participate optimally in the information economy if they were to depend exclusively on household computer access. There is a massive variation in access between the provinces. For example, Gauteng and the

Western Cape have far greater access levels than the third-ranked KwaZulu-Natal (KZN), with Gauteng's percentage virtually double that of KZN.

The analysis suggests that on average 9.1 per cent of all households had access to the Internet in 2003. Note that a household was counted as having Internet access where any household member could access the Internet whether in the dwelling or at another place (for instance at work). This means that if household access was defined in terms of a dedicated household PC with modem, it would consist of a very small number of households. There was a wide range of household access to the Internet across provinces. This was indicated by the fact that households in the Western Cape are seven times more likely to have Internet access than households in Limpopo.

Composite indicators of access to ICT

Composite indicators were developed to capture the overall state of private household access to ICT and public provision of ICT at the municipal level.

Composite indicator 1: Private household access to ICT

The composite indicator on private ICT access was developed from the following variables: access to landline telephones (number of households with access to main telephone lines), number of households with access to mobile telephones, access to computers (number of households with access to personal computers), and access to the Internet (number of households with Internet access).

The development of a composite index is useful because at any one time, people may have the opportunity to use one or more technologies for their purposes. Therefore, if consumers are creating their own combination of ICT use from what is available in their locality, then a measure of the package of facilities that they are able to choose from is important. This index gives a clear overall indication of how people in some municipalities have better access to a wider range of ICT availability than people in other municipalities. In only 12 municipalities are at least one-in-four households able to access all four items (landline, a mobile phone, a computer and the Internet). When these data are presented on a map, the gap in ICT access is revealed to be primarily between the urban centres and the rural periphery. The digital divide is especially visible between the metropolitan areas and the rest of the country.

Composite indicator 2: Public access to ICT

The majority of people in developing countries require publically accessible ICTs through government supplied facilities. This makes measuring public access to community ICT facilities particularly important. In this research report, the following four indicators were identified to capture the overall state of access to public information and telecommunication service centres across the country: Multi-Purpose Community Centres (MPCCs), telecentres and Cyberlabs, libraries, and Public Information Terminals (PITs).

There is a distinct variance across provinces and municipalities in the distribution of ICT service centres. The findings reveal that the overwhelming majority of municipalities have less than two public ICT service centres per 1 000 people. A large number of municipalities – more than 40 – have from zero public ICT service centres to one centre per 1 000 people. The composite indicator on public access to ICT service centres shows that high concentrations of public ICT service centres are found in municipalities that are largely urban as compared to low levels found in municipalities that are largely rural. These differences illustrate the unequal distribution of public ICT service between urban and rural areas.

Recommendations

Arising from this study a number of recommendations were proposed. Four particularly important recommendations are noted here.
- An integrated national ICT information framework: National statistics and data gathering need to be coordinated by putting an integrated ICT information framework in place.
- Understanding household ICT expenditure: It is imperative to investigate average household income in relation to a basket of telecommunication costs and track household expenditure on telecommunications over time. This research will contribute to understanding ICT affordability.
- Targeting of areas needing improvement in ICT penetration: That the Department of Communication, the USAASA and other government agencies such as the Department of Provincial and Local Government consider working with groups or clusters of municipalities that score low on the ICT indexes. This will require further interrogation of the data at the provincial level.
- Monitor access to Community Service Telephones (CSTs): That the USAASA and other agencies monitor the current distribution of CSTs to ensure that the current pattern does not deteriorate. That ICASA (the Independent Communications Authority of South Africa) specify the location of CST rollout where CST provision is part of future telecommunication providers licensing agreements. That existing licence holders' universal access objectives be re-evaluated in the light of the growth in the mobile telephone industry and the continuing need for pro-poor ICT connectivity interventions.

CHAPTER 1

Introduction

1.1 The importance of access to information and communication technologies in South Africa

The current and future capacity of South Africa to generate and sustain access to information and communication technologies (ICTs) for its citizens is an important development priority.

The shape of the South African economy is changing, with the relative emphasis gradually moving away from the primary and manufacturing sectors toward services (the tertiary sector). ICTs contribute to this transformation. As a 'general purpose technology' they play a role in transforming business processes in enterprises, across entire industries. They have impacted on the occupational structure and skills needs in the following ways:
- evolution of new kinds of work (e.g. call centre industry);
- evolution of work outside of the workplace (e.g. tele-work);
- creation of virtual environments for global teamwork and interaction (e.g. Internet, email); and
- job-shedding at the occupational (e.g. typesetting), enterprise (e.g. Business Process Reengineering, robotics, etc.) and industry levels (e.g. travel agency services).

Access to ICTs and ICT skills are therefore critical to working South Africans. But more than this, ICTs support the following fundamental development objectives:
- the promotion of economic growth and development through increased opportunities for employment creation;
- enabling people to identify work opportunities and to take up life-long learning opportunities;
- the consolidation of democracy and human rights through citizens' increased accessibility to information, as well as increased opportunities for communicating freely with each other on matters of civic importance;
- enabling greater transparency and opportunity for citizen feedback to government;
- enabling South Africa's people to seize the opportunity and power to contribute to governance at a grassroots level;
- catalysing local economic development projects (e.g.: e-business development of SMMEs and co-operatives, e-health, e-education); and
- leveraging community resources and promoting social capital through community informatics.

To achieve these development objectives it is necessary to rollout ICT infrastructure on a national basis. This is an aim of government and, more specifically, of the Universal Service and Access Agency of South Africa (USAASA). The USAASA has adopted the first five development objectives given above (USAASA 2004).

The USAASA seeks to provide universal service, denoting 'a reliable connection to the communication network that enables any form of communication to and from any part of South Africa' (USAASA 2004). The organisation also aims to provide universal access to ICTs, which is defined as 'the ability to use the communication network at a reasonable distance and affordable price which provides relevant information and has the necessary capacity – in under-serviced areas' (USAASA 2004). These definitions are provisional and are subject to extensive consultation with relevant stakeholders and approval by the Minister of Communications, as stipulated in the Telecommunications Act of 1996, as amended.

The issues of service and access are of fundamental importance and must apply to all citizens. Unfortunately, there is a significant proportion of the South African population that for reasons of historical discrimination does not have equitable access. Therefore, the mandate of the USAASA requires it to focus in particular on 'under-serviced areas'. These areas are defined as 'communities that live in rural and peri-urban areas that are characterized by poverty, poor infrastructure i.e. telecommunication services, high rate of unemployment and few employment opportunities' (USAASA 2004).

Encouraging universal access is an extremely important function because some people have far greater access to and use of ICTs than others and this is a growing characteristic of the so-called 'information economy'. In his keynote address on 'Information Technology and Global Development' to the Economic and Social Council of the United Nations in May 2000, Professor Manuel Castells warned of inequality, poverty and social exclusion for the South in the new global networked economy (Castells 2000). As the information economy and its associated technologies become more pervasive, it is apparent that, '[the] ability to access, adapt, and create new knowledge using new information and communication technology is critical to social inclusion in today's era' (Warschauer 2003: 9). The problem of social exclusion as it relates to information technology is evident both between and within national contexts (Hendry 2000).

It is critically important to obtain information on the extent of ICT access and use in South Africa so that planning can maximise the opportunities to exploit ICT for improved equity and social and economic development.

Such information is important to the Accelerated and Shared Growth Initiative of South Africa (ASGI-SA), launched by the government in 2006. President Mbeki has identified a group of key factors that are affecting South Africa's drive to achieve 6 per cent economic growth and to halve unemployment and poverty in South Africa by 2014. One of these factors is the cost of telecommunications. The cost of telecommunications is, in turn, a determining aspect of the drive to improve access to ICT in order to overcome the social inequity of the past and to support economic growth.

In addition, information on the extent of ICT use and access will enable agencies such as the USAASA, the Department of Communications and other government, private and NGO bodies to establish the areas of greatest need and to therefore plan and focus investments, projects and scalable programmes accordingly. Furthermore, research information would provide the basis for the elaboration of relevant policy (Gillwald et al. 2005).

1.2 Universal ICT access and service in South Africa since 1994

The political negotiations that led to the first democratic elections in April 1994 were acclaimed as a breakthrough and as an important landmark in the history of South Africa. The event marked a monumental political transformation (Horwitz 1997) and committed the democratic government to a radical restructuring of society, including the political, social, educational, cultural and economic sectors as well as the country's various policies (Butcher 1998). Telecommunications policy was no exception.

An underlying principle guiding the mobilisation of telecommunications for development in South Africa has been the promotion of universal service and universal access. This process of broadening connectivity led to the establishment of the USAASA, which operates under the regulatory and policy framework stipulated in the Telecommunications Act 103 of 1996 (South Africa 1996), as amended in 2001. This Act mandates the USAASA to rollout ICTs in under-serviced areas of South Africa, particularly rural, peri-urban and underdeveloped townships. The main reason behind extending networks into these areas is to ensure that the benefits of the information society do not, as in South Africa's past, flow to particular sections of society only.

One of the present government's immediate priorities when coming into power was to replace previous policies with a set of policy positions that addressed inequalities in all aspects of South African life. In the telecommunications sector, the first objective of the Telecommunications Act 103 of 1996 was to facilitate the universal and affordable provision of telecommunication services (Benjamin 2003). However, the concepts of universal service and universal access differ between countries and regions, as well as within the different contexts of a single country.

The concept of universal service generally refers to all households in a country having a telephone, so that all individuals can make a telephone call from home. Many European and North American countries define universal service based on cost of usage as opposed to network provision. Universal service is taken to refer to three elements: availability, accessibility and affordability.

On the other hand, in a developing country universal access refers to all individuals having reasonable access to a telephone that is either in their own home, at a business, or at some public facility. Universal access is usually defined in terms of specific targets to be reached, for example, access to a phone within a certain travelling distance (Pillay 1998). In South Africa, the 2003–04 Annual Report of the USAASA shows that the goals of universal service and universal access go beyond basic telephony to encompass other advanced services, such as the Internet.

1.3 Indicators of ICT access

In South Africa the effective use of ICTs can serve as a powerful development tool. Furthermore, the country faces the challenge of reducing and ultimately removing the differences in access to ICTs between social groups, thereby extending the benefits of this technology to all sectors of South African society.

In order to develop appropriate strategies and policies to achieve the above, there must be a clear understanding of what conditions currently exist (i.e. where we are now) and what gaps there are (i.e. what we need to do).

Therefore, the pattern according to which ICT access – and usage – is distributed spatially in a country between different areas (e.g. rural–urban), and is distributed demographically between different socio-economic classes (e.g. rich–poor) is of vital importance.

An understanding of ICT distribution in relation to a country's population is possible by using one or more indicators of ICT access. An indicator is a convenient numerical means of expressing or reflecting the state of a phenomenon. Put differently, an indicator is a statistic – or a measure – that can be used as evidence to show change in the behaviour of a particular phenomenon (e.g. change in the number of mobile telephone subscribers). An indicator is defined by the kind of data to be collected, how often the data are to be collected, and how the data are then applied in a calculation to arrive at the indicator.

For instance, it is important to establish how many people have access to a telephone line in a country. If the number of people and the number of telephone lines have been counted, the relationship between these two numbers can be calculated as an indicator. For example, an indicator of access to telephone lines used internationally is the number of telephone lines per 100 or per 1 000 people. This same method can be used to reflect the extent to which people have access to mobile telephones or to the Internet.

It is important to employ internationally standardised indicators so that comparisons can be made between different countries. It is also important to calculate the indicator using the same method each time, as this makes it possible to monitor changes in an indicator between time periods.

There are a number of initiatives that aim to capture ICT indicators in Africa, such as:
- International Telecommunications Union (ITU) World Telecommunication Indicators Database;
- African ICTs Roadmap, supported by the ITU;
- World Economic Forum-Nepad E-Africa Commission's 'E-Readiness' Policy Programme;
- Economic Commission for Africa SCAN-ICT Indicators of ICT: The impact of ICT at the country level;
- *ICT Sector Performance in Africa* reviews published by researchictafrica.net, which is funded by the IDRC; and
- Sub-sectoral initiatives and country initiatives such as Schoolnet Africa, which collaborates with the International Institute for Communication and Development on education-ICT indicators.

An indicator can only be created if the data for that indicator are available. In many countries, moves to capture information that enables the tracking of ICT access and use have only recently been made. Within Africa, there are often data gaps, which make it difficult and sometimes impossible to create indicators using standard international formulae. This information shortfall arises because, in Africa, national statistical agencies may not necessarily collect data on the phenomenon, or the data may not be collected in the required way (e.g. access to telephones may be reported per household rather than per individual), and/or private sector ICT service providers may not be willing to provide data for fear of releasing strategic business intelligence into the public domain. Finally, conducting national censuses to obtain the desired data is an extremely expensive exercise. There may be no private or NGO agencies with the available resources to collect the required information, even through using a less costly household survey approach.

As far as the authors of this report are aware, the only research based on a large-scale survey methodology that has been conducted on ICT access in South Africa recently was undertaken by the LINK Centre of the University of the Witwatersrand in 2004, using a sample of 6 701 individuals living in 1 740 households (Gillwald et al. 2004; Gillwald et al. 2005). This study proved a valuable point of comparison with the data derived from various sources by the Human Sciences Research Council (HSRC) project team.

As a result, indicators must be periodically created from the available data. This is the case with respect to obtaining data for this report. In the medium to long term it will be desirable to obtain the funding, create the infrastructure and develop the methodological processes in order to obtain sustainable statistical measures of ICT access over time.

1.1.1 Complexity underlying analysis of access to ICT

The concept of the digital divide invites us to think of 'haves' and 'have-nots'. However, this approach simplifies a rather more complicated reality. There are many gradations of access to digital resources and many variables that impact on eventual access to and use of ICTs.

Firstly, access to – and use of – ICT facilities involves more than spatial proximity to ICT infrastructure, although the concept of ICT penetration emphasises the spatial and infrastructural aspects of increasing access to this technology. The concept of ICT access is broader and assumes that there are a variety of factors that influence patterns of usage. These factors include education, mobility of individuals, families and communities, and also the user-friendliness and cost of the technologies offered by private enterprises, government and NGOs. This aspect has been stressed by Oyedemi (2005), who suggests that the ultimate aim of universal access is impacted upon by the following: content and language, social relevance of technology, literacy, the technology service platform and the availability of other social utilities.

Secondly, at any one time, people may have the opportunity to use one or more technologies for their purposes. For example, Gillwald, Esselaar, Burton and Stavrou (2005: 139) point out that consumers will use various forms of telephone access – landline, cellphone, public telephone, etc., 'as part of a strategic combination of maximising their tele-expenditure and tele-usage'. If consumers are creating their own combination of ICT use from what is available in their locality, then a measure of the package of facilities that they are able to choose from may be useful. This report will therefore present a set of 'composite indicators'. These indicators combine the set of individual ICT indicators to give an overall indication of how people in some localities will have better access to a wider range of ICT availability than in other localities.

Finally, access to ICT does not necessarily guarantee quality of service. Unfortunately, this analysis cannot take into account the quality of ICT services in terms of: time availability of service (e.g. number of hours a telephone kiosk is open); frequency and period of breakdown of service (e.g. down time of lines and duration of inoperability); and quality (e.g. speed of Internet service). Further research may address the question of quality of service between different technologies, regions and user groups.

1.1.2 Mapping indicators of access

For this project, as undertaken by the HSRC on behalf of the USAASA, data were obtained from ICT service providers and other relevant government data sources. Where national census data were not available per individual or per household for specific indicators, it was necessary to model data obtained from national household survey datasets held by the HSRC, the South African Social Attitudes Survey (SASAS).

For each indicator, modelled data were integrated into a Geographical Information Systems (GIS) analysis and aggregated to the municipality level for further analysis. This provides a picture of the relative difference in access to ICT across the 262 local municipalities in South Africa. In other words, the GIS analysis shows what proportions of the population resident in a particular municipality have access to forms of ICT.

This report, based on the GIS mapping-information capability, therefore makes an important contribution to our understanding of South African spatial dimensions of ICT access between urban, peri-urban and rural areas. The maps in this report provide a visual representation of how particular local authorities are placed in respect to ICT access for their resident populations.

It is hoped that the use of GIS in this research will contribute to an increased level of informed debate on issues such as teledensity – and more broadly ICT access.

1.3.3 The indicators

Based on the available datasets, eleven indicators that most closely corresponded with indicators of ICT access applied internationally were selected.

Related indicators were grouped together for ease of analysis, and refer to:
- access to telecommunications, computers and the Internet in the household;
- access to various forms of public telecommunications service centres;
- access to telecommunications services in areas designated as under-serviced; and
- support to areas hitherto under-serviced regarding access to telecommunications.

In addition to the above, two composite indicators were developed to capture the overall 'state' of ICT access across the country. The two composite indicators were reported at the municipal level.

The list of indicators used in the analysis can be found in Appendix II of this report.

CHAPTER 2

Access to telephonic communications

Improving general access to telephone communications in any society in the 21st century will bring economic, social and political benefits to that society. As an instrument of communication, the ways in which the telephone contributes to the lives of individuals, families, businesses, governments and the broader civil society is immense, as the following examples will attest:

- A small rural farmer calls the markets to find the best price for produce to maximise the profitability of his/her business.
- The principal of a school calls the district manager to postpone his/her visit as the local roads are impassable in the rain.
- A young man living in the city calls his illiterate mother in a deep rural settlement to tell her about his new job.
- A woman at a clinic calls a hospital to summon an ambulance and saves the life of an injured child.
- A corporate executive convenes a teleconference with managers spread across the continent to discuss an important decision.
- A student calls her classmate to discuss the interpretation of an assignment.
- A recent university graduate living in an informal settlement outside of Johannesburg is able to arrange a job interview without incurring significant travel costs.

Telephonic interactions provide a relatively fast, efficient and reliable means of communication and bring people together in many ways. However, telephonic communication is a service that carries a cost. In some countries, telecommunications providers may not be in a position to provide universal coverage because of demographic, geographic or technological factors; or the local market may not offer telecommunications services at a price that is affordable to all those who might need or want it. Government may not have the resources or the political will to regulate the telecommunications sector in ways that make access to telephone communications sufficiently cheap to allow universal access. The pattern of access to telephone communications is influenced by national policies and global pressures, which strongly influence the shape of the local market.

Over and above issues of market regulation and competition, the global telephone communications market is becoming increasingly complex as new technologies (wired and wireless) become available. For example, mobile/cellular telephony revolutionised the field, which hitherto had relied mainly on wired and optical fibre-based telephony. A strong influence on telephone communications in the future is likely to arise out of the application of Voice Over Internet Protocol (VOIP). Unit cost profiles of the different telephone technologies differ quite considerably as a result of market and technological factors. As a result, these cost profiles directly affect access and affordability.

In 2004 the incumbent fixed-line operator, Telkom, had 4.8 million subscribers. However, according to Gillwald et al. (2005), Telkom suffered a decline in its subscriber base since 2000, which can mainly be ascribed to price increases enforced by the operator. Telkom recently re-stated its fixed-line figures in its *2005 Annual Report*, which suggests that fixed-line figures may not necessarily have declined since 2002. In the same period, the pace of growth in the rollout of fixed lines, especially to rural and under-serviced areas, has been slow. By way of contrast, in 2004 the total number of cellphone subscribers was approximately 19 million, demonstrating how cellphone usage has compensated for poor fixed-line access. This figure, however, is also subject to debate: there appears to be no agreed-upon definition of mobile subscribers, causing telecommunications analysts to suggest that the number claimed is overstated by as much as 20 per cent.

By 2005, more than 94 per cent of the South African population lived and worked within cellphone coverage areas (Knott-Craig 2005), which means that the cellphone networks provide more comprehensive coverage than Telkom. Even though cellphone costs are higher than the fixed-line costs offered by Telkom, it could be argued that the use of cellphones is a forced 'choice' because of a lack of alternatives. There is evidence that low-income users are using cellphones that they cannot really afford or using money for this purpose that should be allocated to other forms of household expenses (Sithole 2004). Gillwald et al. (2005) observe that poorer mobile users are in certain circumstances prepared to sacrifice food for airtime because they view their cellphones as essential to their survival. Mobile users adapt as best they can to this situation by using free SMSs, 'please call me's, 'buzzing' or resorting to other connectivity sources such as public telephones when rates are cheaper.

The telecommunications data discussed in this report refer to: telephone lines, cellular telephones and community service telephones (CST). Each of these three forms of telephone service has a particular profile of users, which is a function of the rollout of fixed and mobile services across the landscape and a function of the relative cost of a unit call. It remains to be seen how the award of a second licence in the fixed-line sector will affect the levels of access among low-income clients. Given the structure of the South African telecommunications market, there is unlikely to be any impact on low-income users (Esselaar & Stork 2005).

2.1 Fixed telephone lines available

The 2001 Telecommunications Bill defines universal access as 'everyone in the country being able to access a telephone within reasonable distance' (cited in Sithole 2004: 3).

Universal service can be measured with reference to (a) ownership by an individual, (b) ownership within a household, or (c) with reference to whether individuals report being able to access a phone within a reasonable distance of the household. This indicator refers to household access – as in (c) – and is based on data from the HSRC SASAS survey undertaken in 2003.

2.1.1 Indicator 1: Access to telephone landlines per household

As shown in Figure 2.2, fixed-line rollout concentrates on urban areas where the general infrastructure and population density is higher.

A critical access factor is the affordability of telecommunication costs. In urban areas more than three-quarters of households spend over a R100 per month on fixed-line communications, with an average spend of R200 per month. In comparison, almost three-quarters of households in rural areas spend less than a R100 per month on fixed-line communications, with a median spend of R35 per month (Gillwald et al. 2004; Gillwald et al. 2005). It is important to look into average household income in relation to fixed-line communication costs in order to address telecommunications accessibility.

Provincial level

The national average household access to fixed-line telephony of 23.6 per cent obtained from the HSRC's SASAS survey of 2003 falls within the range of the 2001 National Census figure of 24.4 per cent and the 2004 study of Gillwald et al. (2005), which obtained a 22.1 per cent average.

In three provinces (the Western Cape, KwaZulu-Natal and Gauteng) the percentage of households with access to fixed lines is higher than the national average. Limpopo has an exceptionally low average access compared to the other provinces.

Table 2.1: Household access to landlines by province

Province	Percentage of households with access to landlines
Western Cape	55.3
KwaZulu-Natal	31.7
Gauteng	28.5
Free State	21.8
Northern Cape	20.0
Mpumalanga	17.6
Eastern Cape	15.9
North West	15.0
Limpopo	7.1
National average	23.6

Source: Data from HSRC (2003)

At the provincial level landline access is unevenly distributed, with higher concentrations of landline access in urban areas and metropoles which have better infrastructure and higher average income levels. Certain provinces have higher proportions of their population residing in urban or metropolitan areas, such as Gauteng, and consequently may have higher average levels of access to telephone communications (Table 2.1). The articulation of population size, density, agglomeration, and population income levels affects access to landlines in different ways. This can be seen from the provincial rank order of percentage of households with access to fixed telephone lines:

- Highest concentration of landlines: Western Cape households have significantly higher access – at double the national average – although the province is home to only a fifth (10.19 per cent) of the national population (Quantec 2004);
- Second ranked: KwaZulu-Natal has the largest share of the national population (20.89 per cent) (Quantec 2004) and second highest household access to landlines. Access is strongly concentrated in the eThekwini metropole and the Msunduzi municipality;
- Third ranked: Gauteng has the second largest population in South Africa (19.47 per cent) (Quantec 2004);
- Fourth ranked: the Free State has the second smallest population (5.96 per cent) and the second lowest population density in South Africa (Quantec 2004);

- Fifth ranked: the Northern Cape has the smallest population in the country (1.87 per cent) (Quantec 2004);
- Sixth ranked: Mpumalanga is home to 6.94 per cent of South Africa's population (Quantec 2004).
- Seventh ranked: the Eastern Cape has the third largest population in South Africa (14.56 per cent) (Quantec 2004);
- Eighth ranked: the North West has the sixth highest population in the country (8.2 per cent) (Quantec 2004);
- Ninth ranked: Limpopo has the least access to landlines, but the fourth largest population in the country (11.92 per cent).

Municipalities

The histogram in Figure 2.1 shows the distribution of municipalities according to the percentage of households within their boundaries that have access to landlines. This ranges from a handful of municipalities where less than 3.5 per cent of the resident population has access to landlines to the other end of the spectrum where, in eleven municipalities, more than 45 per cent of the population has access to landlines. The overwhelming majority of municipalities have landline access ranging between 3.5 per cent and 25 per cent, with a large group located between 3.5 per cent and 8.5 per cent. Towards the higher end of the 3.5 to 25 per cent range there is a visible clumping of municipalities, with another peak at the 16.5 per cent household access level.

Figure 2.1: Number of municipalities with percentage of households having landline access

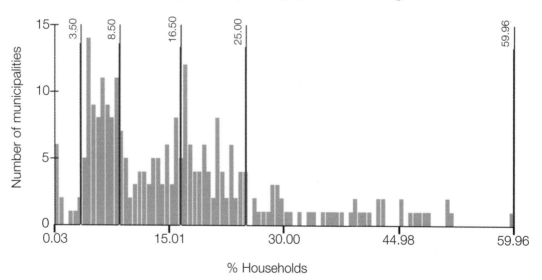

Landlines are concentrated in the metropoles and major cities where good infrastructure and higher household income levels exist, such as Cape Town, Port Elizabeth, Durban, Pietermaritzburg, Kimberley, Johannesburg, and Pretoria. In these cities, between 25.01 per cent and 59.96 per cent of households have access to landlines.

In municipalities located in rural areas, where the majority of people are black and have a low household income, only 0.03 per cent to 3.50 per cent of households have access to landlines. Examples of these municipalities include Kagiso Municipality and Moshaweng Municipality in the North West, Umhlabuyalingana Municipality in KwaZulu-

Natal, Maruleng Municipality in Limpopo, and Bushbuckridge Municipality in Mpumalanga (Figure 2.2).

Figure 2.2: Percentage of households with access to landlines per municipality

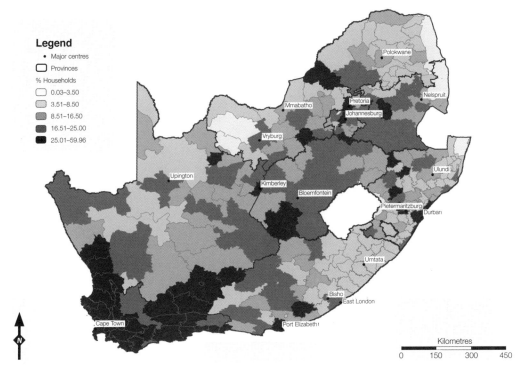

Source: Data from HSRC (2003)

2.2 Cellular subscribers

In 1992, only 1 in 237 people worldwide used a mobile phone; a decade later this had soared to 1 in 5 (WorldWatch Institute 2004). South Africa has made significant progress towards universal telephone access because of the huge uptake of cellphones, both through private ownership and via the establishment of phone shops (Benjamin 2002). This discussion will focus on private access to cellphones. The International Telecommunication Union (ITU) reported that from a base of just under one million subscribers in 1996, the number of mobile subscribers in South Africa overtook fixed-line subscribers in 1999. According to the most recent figures from *Business Report* (9 January 2006), Vodacom stands at 17.5 million subscribers, MTN at 10 million and Cell C at 2.7 million. This estimation would vary according to the definition of subscribers that is applied.

Access to cellphones for the low-income sectors of the population has opened up, mainly through the pre-paid option, as opposed to a contract that stipulates income and other prerequisites for qualification. Most mobile telephones are pre-paid phones (81.2 per cent), while slightly more than one-in-ten (13.6 per cent) are contract, and a further 1.3 per cent are likely to be purchased by a company or business (Gillwald et al. 2005). In rural areas, 97 per cent of cellphones are used on a pre-paid basis (Gillwald et al. 2004).

Mobile operators that use digital networks report strong growth in the number of subscribers. Vodacom had around 57 per cent of subscribers in South Africa; MTN, around a third of subscribers; and Cell C around 10 per cent of subscribers in 2005 (Burrows 2005). In 2005, around 93 per cent of corporations in South Africa indicated that they intended to deploy cellphones among staff in 2005 (World Wide Worx 2005).

Increases in telephonic penetration have been achieved through cellphones despite high mobile call charges. The high call charges are a reflection of the weak regulatory systems in place (Gillwald 2005).

2.2.1 Indicator 2: Access to cellphones

The use of cellphone technologies in South Africa has made it possible to service rural areas at a lower cost than that of installing fixed lines (Economist Intelligence Unit 2005). However, because densely populated black South African townships make the marketing of services relatively easy and prove more profitable to cover than rural areas, operators have focused most of their efforts in the former areas (Benjamin 2002).

Provincial level
The provinces are ranked below in order of level of household cellphone access (Table 2.2).

Five provinces (Gauteng, Western Cape, North West, KwaZulu-Natal and the Free State) have a higher average household access to cellphones than the national average. Four provinces (Mpumalanga, Limpopo, Eastern Cape and the Northern Cape) are below the national household average.

Table 2.2: Household access to cellular phones by province

Province	Percentage of households with access to cellphones
Gauteng	48.7
Western Cape	46.7
North West	35.3
KwaZulu-Natal	35.2
Free State	33.9
Mpumalanga	26.3
Limpopo	26.1
Eastern Cape	25.7
Northern Cape	20.1
National average	33.1

Source: Data from HSRC (2003)

Data on provincial access indicate that mobile technologies enable services to be provided to both densely populated areas and rural areas.

Comparing cellphone and landline access figures, Table 2.3 shows that the average household access to cellphones is higher than the average access to landlines. This is the case for all the provinces except for the Western Cape, where landline access is approximately 8 per cent higher than cellphone access.

The usage of cellphones is around 20 per cent higher in Gauteng and the North West, and 19 per cent higher in Limpopo. Both high cellphone and landline usage in Gauteng could possibly be attributed to a higher income level in the province than in other provinces. The high cellphone uptake in the North West and Limpopo could possibly be attributed to relatively low fixed-line availability in these provinces. Further analysis would be needed to establish the conditions that give rise to these patterns. However, the influence of a variety of factors – household income, availability of landlines, population density, market size – or a combination of these and other factors could be the probable cause.

Table 2.3: Comparison of household access to telephone communications by province

Province	Percentage households with cellphone	Percentage households with landline	Difference in percentage
Gauteng	48.7	28.5	20.2
Western Cape	46.7	55.3	-8.6
North West	35.3	15.0	20.3
KwaZulu-Natal	35.2	31.7	3.5
Free State	33.9	21.8	12.1
Mpumalanga	26.3	17.6	8.7
Limpopo	26.1	7.1	19.0
Eastern Cape	25.7	15.9	9.8
Northern Cape	20.1	20.0	0.1
National average	33.1	23.6	9.5

Source: Data from HSRC (2003)

Municipalities

The histogram in Figure 2.3 shows the distribution of municipalities according to the percentage of households within their boundaries which have access to cellular phones. Noticeably, in the majority of municipalities, between 20 and 30 per cent of the resident population have access to cellular phones. Further, in a relatively large number of municipalities, access to cellular phones is between 30 and 40 per cent. This reveals that generally municipalities have higher levels of cellular phone access than landline access and corroborates the national averages shown in Table 2.2.

Figure 2.3: Number of municipalities with percentage of households having access to cellular phones

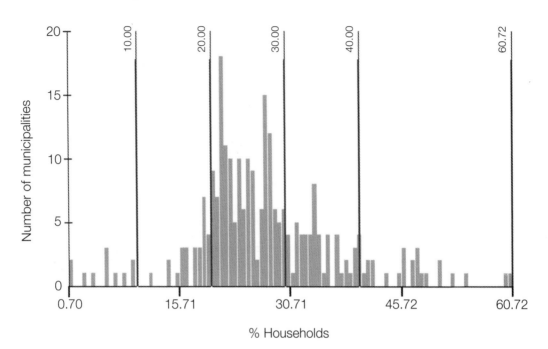

There is a set of municipalities where relatively high levels of household cellular phone access – between 40.01 and 60.72 per cent – were evident in 2003. These municipalities showed high concentrations of urban economic activity, or were located in tourism-intensive areas (Figure 2.4):
- Johannesburg Metropole, which contributed around 12.94 per cent to South Africa's GDP (Quantec 2003);
- Cape Town Metropole (2006), which contributed around 11.01 per cent to the country's GDP (Quantec 2003) and was chosen as the Best City in Africa in 2004;
- Tshwane Metropole, which contributed 8.34 per cent to GDP (Quantec 2003);
- Kopanong Municipality, which contributed around 42.4 per cent to the economy of Xhariep (2006);
- Emnambithi-Ladysmith Municipality, which boasts various cultural attractions;
- Mossel Bay Municipality (the historical capital of the Garden Route); and
- Oudtshoorn Municipality (famous for the Cango Caves).

In contrast, there are a number of municipalities that have relatively low levels of household access to cellphones. In several municipalities an average of between 5 and 15 per cent of households – or at best one in five – had access to cellphones. These municipalities also tend to be poorer. The municipalities are:
- Tsolwana and Inkwanca Municipalities, situated in the Eastern Cape in the Oliver Tambo District Municipality, where 81.5 per cent of the population lives in poverty (Global Insight 2004); and
- Mbizana Municipality, set in the Chris Hani District Municipality of the Eastern Cape, where 75.7 per cent of the population lives in poverty (Global Insight 2004).

ACCESS TO TELEPHONIC COMMUNICATIONS

Figure 2.4: Household access to cellular phones per municipality

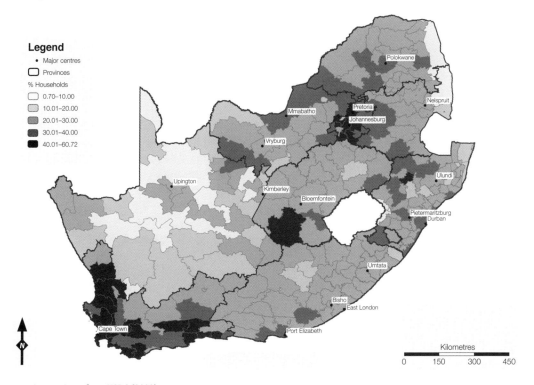

Source: Data from HSRC (2003)

2.2.2 Analysis of access to cellphones based on data from cellphone service providers

The data discussed above were drawn from the HSRC's SASAS household survey (2003) and therefore reflects the telephone access conditions as reported by respondents. It was considered to be important to compare the data reported above with the data provided by the cellphone service providers.

A comparison of access to cellphones based on data obtained from service providers (Cell C, MTN, Vodacom) provided a very different picture to that obtained from the household survey discussed above. This was because cellphones were counted where they were being used – given the position of the cellphone (actually its SIM card) as tracked/identified by each network provider. The position of the cellphone bore no necessary relation to the home address of the user, due to the inherent mobility of both cellphones and cellphone owners.

When the data on cellphone user location was compared to data on the household residence of the population, anomalies arose. Calculating ratios of cellphones per 1 000 people on the basis of actual cellphone location produced irregular data, especially in highly mobile populations where people have to commute to work each day.

There are therefore limits to the usefulness of analysing data from service providers for the construction of an indicator of access where cellphones (or SIM-card data) are not linked to individual owners and their place of residence. Given that the majority of users obtained services by means of ad hoc pre-paid methods, there is by definition no means of establishing their place of residence. Data from service providers in the format provided do not suit the requirements of the indicator-based analysis undertaken in this report. For these reasons, full discussion of the results based on cellphone provider information is not presented in the body of this report, but may be found in Appendix 1.

2.3 Community Service Telephones

In many developing countries, telecommunication access through Community Service Telephones (CSTs) is a primary form of access. In South Africa, CSTs are public access payphones in under-serviced areas, as designated by the USAASA. In terms of their licence obligations, telecommunications service providers are obliged to rollout CSTs. All CSTs rolled out – whether cellular or fixed-line – are payphones. Service providers use different methods of providing access, such as 'phone shops', kiosks and portable telephones. Providers also train CST operators.

For the period May 1997 to May 2002, Telkom was obliged to rollout 120 000 CST payphones, while the mobile service providers MTN and Vodacom were obliged to install 7 500 and 22 000 CSTs respectively in the same period. The intention was that the CST service should also be provided at a low community service tariff. These obligations were achieved in the stipulated period and exceeded in the case of the cellular service providers.

However, the placement of phones by the providers may not necessarily have been optimal for extending service, because it was not effectively controlled or monitored (Hodge 2004). A third mobile phone service provider, Cell C, was licensed in November 2001 under the obligation to rollout 52 000 CSTs over a seven-year period (Sithole 2004). The data given in Table 2.4 refer only to 2005 data on CST service provision by cellular telephone providers.

Table 2.4: Provision of CSTs by cellular telephone service providers per province, 2005

Province	Number of CSTs
Eastern Cape	8 205
Free State	6 008
Gauteng	21 123
KwaZulu-Natal	12 521
Limpopo	9 272
Mpumalanga	5 485
Northern Cape	850
North West	4 755
Western Cape	5 791
Total	74 010

Source: Cell C, MTN, Vodacom 2005

The following discussion first introduces the CST rollout in terms of total numbers of CSTs per municipality. Thereafter, a measure is created that represents the number of CSTs in relation to the population per municipality – as Indicator 3.

2.3.1 Community Service Telephones connected per municipality

Please note that the following analysis is based on CST data given to the HSRC by the mobile telephone providers. Telkom did not supply data on their CST rollout.

The histogram in Figure 2.5 shows that about 125 municipalities have less than 60 CSTs located within their boundaries and that the majority of municipalities have less than 500 CSTs. A very small number (six municipalities) have more than 1 800 CSTs within their boundaries. The rollout of CSTs is clearly uneven at the municipal level.

Figure 2.5: Number of municipalities by number of CSTs

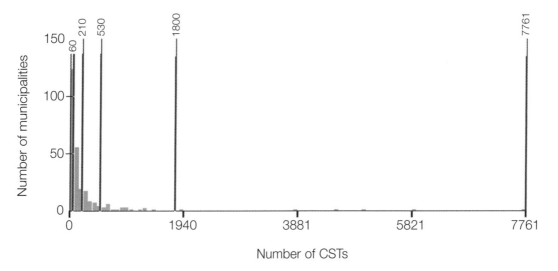

Even though the overall rollout targets for CST by cellular telephone service providers seem to have been met, the CSTs may not have been placed where most needed, as shown in Figure 2.6. Large areas of the Northern Cape, the Western Cape and the Eastern Cape, as well as parts of KwaZulu-Natal and the Free State have the lowest range (0 – 60) of CSTs available. Many of these areas are remote and have a low population density. Areas with the highest numbers of CSTs (1 991 – 7 761) per municipal area are:
- Cape Town in the Western Cape;
- Durban in KwaZulu-Natal;
- Johannesburg and Pretoria in Gauteng; and
- Thulamela Municipality in Limpopo.

This suggests that CSTs are concentrated in areas with a high population density, offering the least cost to service providers. However, in many areas where population density is low and where there are low per-capita-income communities there is poor access to CSTs. This is contrary to the aim of providing CSTs, and the regulatory authority should monitor rollout more effectively so that the objective of greater access can be achieved.

Figure 2.6: Number of CSTs per municipality

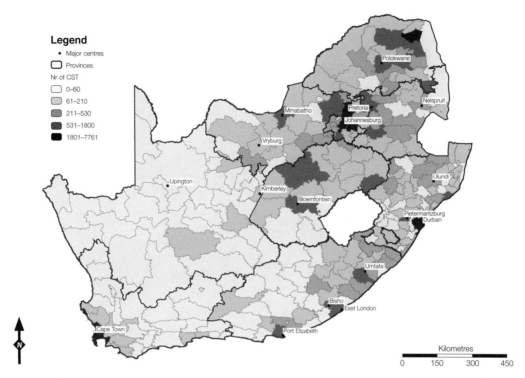

2.3.2 Indicator 3: Number of Community Service Telephones per 1 000 people

It is important to observe that the number of CSTs per unit of population – as provided by cellular telephone service providers – is very small. The majority of municipalities have between 0.16 and 1.70 CSTs per 1 000 people. About one third of municipalities has less than one CST per 1 000 people. Only ten municipalities have four or more CSTs per 1 000 people, a ratio of 1:250 people available for public use (see Figure 2.7)

Figure 2.7: Number of municipalities by number of CSTs per 1 000 people

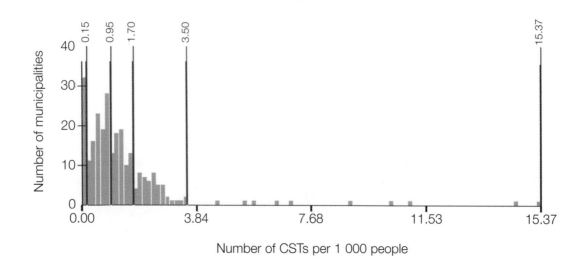

Access to telephonic communications

Of particular interest is the extent to which the spatial distribution of CST rollout has met under-serviced areas and populations. Immediately apparent from the map in Figure 2.8 is the concentration of CST provision in two main regions: i) municipalities within a 200 km range of the Johannesburg-Pretoria axis, and ii) in the central and eastern parts of Limpopo Province. On balance, the Eastern Cape seems to have the lowest overall coverage apart from one or two higher density municipalities.

None of the areas with the most CSTs per 1 000 people (3.51 to 15.37) are metropolitan municipal authorities. For example:
- District Municipality 18 (Masilonyana, Tokologo, Tswelopele, Matjhabeng, and Nala Municipalities) in the Free State;
- Diamondfields (NCDMA09), Thembelihle Municipality, and Kareeberg Municipality in the Northern Cape;
- Sisonke Municipality in KwaZulu-Natal; and
- Aberdeen Plain (ECDMA10) in the Eastern Cape.

Areas with only 0.00 to 0.15 CSTs per 1 000 people are, for example:
- Mier Municipality, Kamiesberg Municipality, Namaqualand Municipality (NCDMA06), Hantam Municipality, Karoo Hoogland Municipality, Renosterberg Municipality, and Siyancuma Municipality in the Northern Cape;
- Central Karoo District Council, Prince Albert Municipality, Oudshoorn Municipality, Langeberg Municipality, and South Cape District Council in the Western Cape;
- Baviaans Municipality, Ikwezi Municipality, and Nxuba Municipality in the Eastern Cape;
- The Big Five False Bay Municipality, and Giants' Castle Game Reserve in KwaZulu-Natal;
- Pilansberg National Park in the North West; and
- John Ness Nature Reserve in Gauteng.

Figure 2.8: Number of CSTs per 1 000 people per municipality

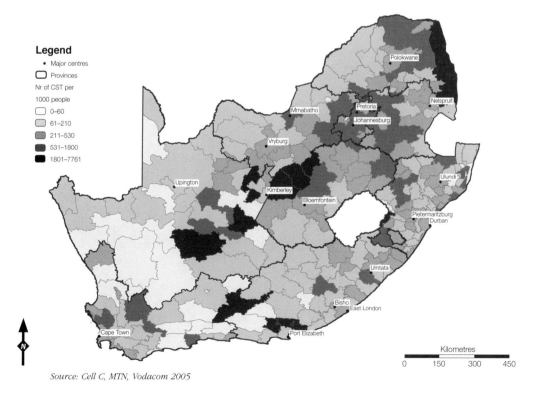

Source: Cell C, MTN, Vodacom 2005

It must be noted that the above analysis is based only on data provided by the mobile telephone service providers. Had Telkom provided their CST data, the number of CSTs to be taken into account in the analysis would have more than doubled. However, given the low base of CST provision, even doubling the numbers would not have improved access to CSTs to a significant degree. The location of Telkom's CSTs according to municipality would probably impact on the spatial distribution of CSTs, but we cannot know whether this is working to the advantage of rural or urban populations.

CHAPTER 3

Access to computers and the Internet

3.1 Access to computers

This indicator refers to access to personal computers (PCs) that are either freestanding, or linked into a network. In a business and home or personal environment, a PC can act as a powerful productivity tool for the following: the creation of documents (word processor, spreadsheet, etc.) and presentations; multimedia creation and editing (of data, text, images, audio or video); scheduling and organisation of time and tasks; manipulating and analysing data; programming; playing games, and for other purposes. Over and above the software that makes the above tasks possible, the PC can be used to run various forms of software (not written by the user) for a range of purposes. Finally, if it has hardware such as a CD-ROM drive or other means of accessing data, the PC can be used to search for, select and retrieve information.

In a business environment, the employee will use the workstation (PC) – which is usually linked into a network – to fulfil her or his job functions. Employees may work in the following ICT-enabled fields: accounting/finance, enterprise applications, programming, data services, databases, call centres, electronic publishing, Internet and web development, networking, hardware and operating systems, and so on.

As the PC becomes a 'workdesk' in many business environments, there is a gradual application of ICT in workplaces across all sectors of the economy. Furthermore, as more and more people use PCs for their own, private purposes, the productive capabilities of this technology assume an increasing importance in the personal domain, alongside its role as an efficient workplace facility.

However, people must in the first instance have access to PCs before they can exercise, practise and extend these skills. The issue of access crucially affects the extent to which people can exploit ICT to their advantage. With no or restricted access, relegation to the other side of the digital divide is likely.

Corporate South Africa regards the laptop computer as the single most necessary mobile technology for deployment in business, edging out even the cellphone (World Wide Worx, Cell C & First National Bank 2005). By way of contrast, the price of PCs remains a barrier to private access to ICT for the majority of the population (World Wild Worx, Razor's Edge Business Intelligence & Trigrammic 2005). Between 1998 and 2001 the proportion of PCs per 1 000 working people in South Africa, including access to a PC at the workplace, was estimated to have increased to over 50 per cent (Economist Intelligence Unit 2005).

3.1.1 Indicator 4: Access to computers per household

Gillwald et al. (2004) report from their survey that 12 per cent of households in South Africa owned a PC, which broadly corresponds with the HSRC finding that 13.6 per cent of households have access to a PC. Clearly, most citizens would therefore not be able to participate optimally in the information economy if they were to depend exclusively on household computer access.

Provincial level

There is a massive variation in PC access between the provinces (Table 3.1). For example, Gauteng and the Western Cape have far greater access levels than the third-ranked KwaZulu-Natal (KZN) province, with Gauteng's percentage virtually double that of KZN. Furthermore, seven provinces have a lower average access than the national average. Particularly troubling is the low level of computer access in Limpopo.

Table 3.1: Percentage of household access to PCs by province

Province	Percentage
Western Cape	33.8
Gauteng	25.2
KwaZulu-Natal	13.3
Free State	10.3
North West	9.9
Northern Cape	9.8
Eastern Cape	7.9
Mpumalanga	7.6
Limpopo	4.4
National average	13.6

Source: Data from HSRC (2003)

The more urbanised and economically developed provinces have higher household access to computers. The Western Cape is campaigning to lead in terms of technology (CITI & WESGRO 2001), followed by Gauteng, the primary economic hub of the South African economy. In other provinces PC access is highest in urban centres such as:
- Upington, Northern Cape;
- Nelspruit and the Highland Municipality, Mpumalanga; and
- Bela Bela Municipality, Limpopo.

Municipalities

At the municipal level, access to computers in households ranges from 0 per cent to about 50 per cent. In most municipalities between 1.75 and 7.75 per cent of households have access to a PC. This means that in very few municipalities – about 30 – is there a more than a one-in-ten household PC access pattern.

Access to computers and the Internet

Figure 3.1: Number of municipalities with percentage of households having access to PCs

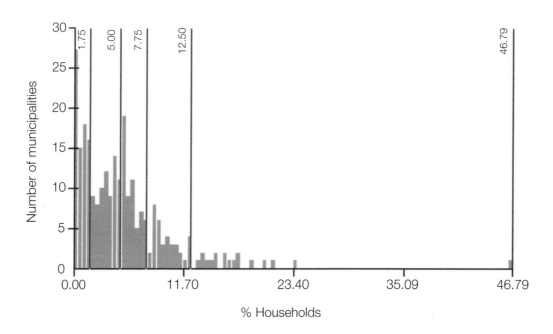

In the following more urbanised municipalities about 12.51 to 46.79 per cent of households have access to PCs: Johannesburg, Pretoria, Durban, Pietermaritzburg, the Highland Municipality, Cape Town, Newcastle Municipality (with the Iscor steel plant), Utrecht Municipality (with coal-mining activities), Sishen (which accounts for 4 per cent of the global seaborne iron ore trade) and other municipalities especially in the Western Cape (Figure 3.2).

There are several municipalities where only 2 in every 100 households or less (0 to 2 per cent of households) have access to a PC; for example, in the Makhado Municipality (in Limpopo); Sisonke Municipality (in KwaZulu-Natal), and other areas, as indicated in Figure 3.2. It is important to note that even if households do have a computer, maintenance and repair of computers in rural areas – as well as travel and time costs – represents a major drain on household resources (Benjamin 2002).

Figure 3.2: Household access to PCs per municipality

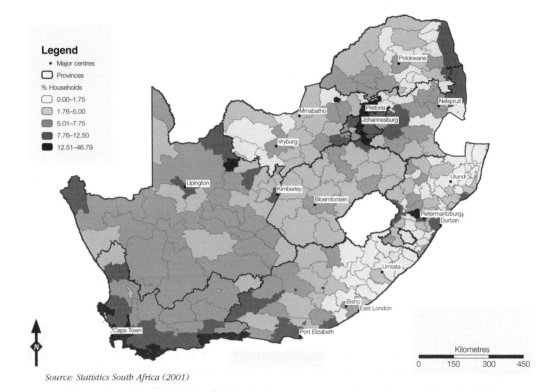

Source: Statistics South Africa (2001)

3.2 Access to the Internet

Access to the Internet is possible via a range of networked devices including: 3G mobile telephones, Personal Digital Assistants (PDAs), and desktop and laptop PCs. Essentially, Internet access is used for sending messages with or without attachments (email), for web browsing, and for interacting in various Internet-based forums. More recently, VOIP protocol enables telecommunications access on the Internet.

Stand-alone PCs themselves are not an information service. In South Africa, Internet access is, however, mainly obtained through PCs. This means that this indicator is to some extent related to the previous indicator – access to a PC.

Access to the Internet enables a range of communication, information-seeking, interactive or educational activities, provides significant opportunities for adding value in the lives of adults and youth, while also contributing to household livelihoods. Household members benefit from Internet access in the following ways:
- communicating for business and personal purposes;
- finding information on the best products and services;
- obtaining information to improve personal investment and financial management;
- accessing medical information;
- obtaining information on current affairs, weather conditions, entertainment, etc.;
- conducting relationships and interacting in communities; and
- enrolling and participating in distance education programmes.

Those with access to the informational resources of the Internet can significantly benefit in the following dimensions: social, financial, educational, recreational and health.

3.2.1 Indicator 5: Access to the Internet per household

In the 1990s, access to the Internet increased dramatically. In global terms, 1992 saw only 1 in 778 people using the Internet, by 2002 that figure had risen to 1 in 10 (WorldWatch Institute 2004). However, only about 682 people per 10 000 inhabitants in South Africa used the Internet in 2002 (Guislain et al. 2005).

Growth in Internet access among the South African public has slowed to the extent that in 2005 the dial-up market experienced no growth in subscribers for the first time since the industry was launched in 1993 (Goldstuck 2005). According to Gillwald et al. (2004 4 per cent of households had a working Internet connection at home, while around 5.7 per cent had an email address. Approximately 75 per cent of South Africans have never used the Internet (Levin 2005).

The number of individual South Africans with Internet access nonetheless increased to 5 per cent in 2005, due to the solid growth in corporate usage and the dramatic uptake of broadband in the private sector (Goldstuck 2005). The impact of broadband, or high-speed Internet access, has been felt more strongly among existing users migrating from dial-up usage than among new users coming online. However, in comparison to other lower-middle income countries, South Africa has a relatively undeveloped broadband market (Gillwald et al. 2004).

There are various levels of Internet connectivity available, incorporating differential price structures based on quality and speed. Affordability is the main issue for those who are still not connected. A key concern is that as long as dial-up access charges and line rentals remain high, and noting that these comprise the bulk of Internet access costs (approximately 80 per cent in 2004), Internet penetration in South Africa will remain stunted (Gillwald et al. 2004).

Provincial level

On a national basis, the 2003 survey upon which this study is based suggests that, on average, 9.1 per cent of all households have access to the Internet, compared to the 4 per cent given in the South African 2004 e-Index produced by the LINK Centre (Gillwald et al. 2004). In both surveys, households were counted as having Internet access where any household member could gain access to the Internet whether in the dwelling or at another place (for instance, at work). This means that household access as defined in terms of a PC with modem in the home is a limited portion of the total.

There is variable household access to the Internet across provinces, as indicated by the fact that households in the Western Cape are seven times more likely to have Internet access than households in Limpopo (Table 3.2). Internet access is highly concentrated in Gauteng and the Western Cape, each of which has double the household access levels of other provinces. By far the lowest level of access is visible in Limpopo, where household access is one third of the national average. The general finding that higher Internet access exists in provinces with higher average income levels highlights the close association between these two factors.

Internet access is mainly concentrated in the larger cities. The two provinces with the highest household access are both characterised by the range of interventions under way to leverage business activity and competitiveness through improving Internet access. For example, one of the Western Cape government's explicit aims is to become a leader in terms of technology, business and infrastructure development. In 2001 Cape Town, in conjunction with UUNET SA, developed the Bandwidth Barn, which is an incubator for small and medium ICT businesses. Gauteng boasts 3 500 small ICT companies (Zaaiman 2004) and a recent SMME survey indicated that SMMEs view Internet connectivity as impacting greatly on competitiveness (Standard Bank, MWEB Business & Microsoft 2005). ICT infrastructure development in Gauteng forms part of a R50 billion plan for accommodating the 2010 World Cup football matches to be hosted in the province (Canada High Commission Trade Office 2005).

The data suggests that areas of high tourist concentration may contribute to demand for more local Internet links and traffic. The speed and extent of Internet access will be influenced by the ICT development plans of local government. For example, the Knysna Municipality, as a local authority, is pioneering the development of a wireless Internet zone, which may generate concepts and guiding principles for other municipalities to adopt in the future.

Table 3.2: Household access to the Internet by province

Province	Percentage of households with access to the Internet
Western Cape	23.4
Gauteng	20.0
KwaZulu-Natal	8.2
Free State	7.3
Mpumalanga	5.5
Eastern Cape	5.5
North West	5.0
Northern Cape	3.9
Limpopo	3.0
National average	9.1

Source: Data from HSRC (2003)

Municipalities
Among South African municipalities, household access to the Internet ranged from under 1 per cent to almost 27 per cent. The histogram in Figure 3.3 shows that in the case of more than 50 municipalities there are negligible proportions of households with access to the Internet. In approximately one third of municipalities, less than 1.25 per cent of households have access to the Internet. Fewer than 50 municipalities show household Internet access exceeding 10 per cent.

Figure 3.3: Number of municipalities with percentage of households having access to the Internet

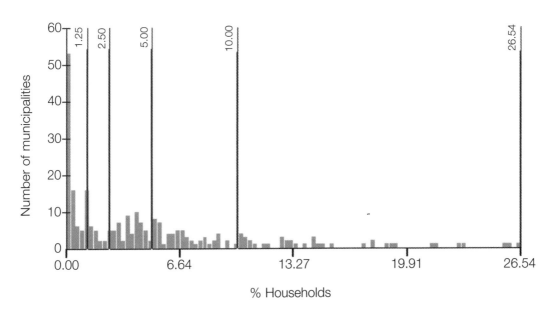

The Western Cape had the highest number of municipalities within the highest band of access, followed by Gauteng. In these municipalities, access ranged from one in every ten to one in every four households.

The metropolitan municipalities enjoying household Internet access from 10.01 per cent to 26.54 per cent include Johannesburg, Pretoria, Durban, Pietermaritzburg, the Highlands Municipality (Mpumalanga), Cape Town and Port Elizabeth. Smaller urban centres such as Mussina, Bela-Bela and Potchefstroom, as well as some rural municipalities, also have relatively high household Internet access levels; for example, Makana Municipality in the Western Cape, which hosts various government department district offices and is a base for pottery and ostrich farming activities. Various municipalities in the Western Cape benefit from tourism, which may explain their higher Internet access index. Analysis of Internet access and other ICT indicators at local levels will uncover explanations for variations in access between municipal authorities.

In many rural municipalities, between 0 and 1.25 per cent of households had access to the Internet (Figure 3.4). These included: Thulamela, Makhado, Moses Kotane, Molopo, Umhlabuyalinga, Mbizana, Tsolwana, and substantial areas of the Eastern Cape, KwaZulu-Natal and Limpopo.

Figure 3.4: Household access to the Internet per municipality

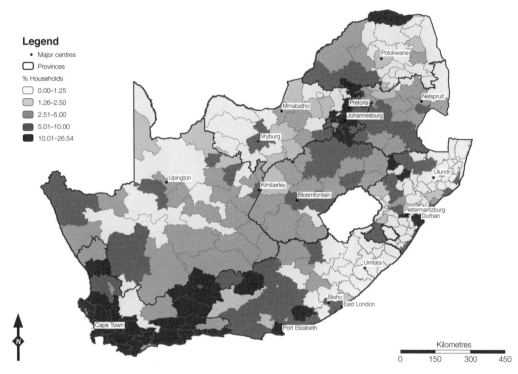

Source: Data from HSRC (2003)

CHAPTER 4

Access to information and telecommunications service centres

Uneven development of the global 'information society' has placed the provision of access to ICT services on the international development agenda. In developing countries, the increasing demand for information and communication services finds expression in long waiting lists for telephone connections, increased use of cellular telephone systems and growing number of Internet users. However, widespread access to these services on an individual basis is simply out of the question in the frame within which policy and strategic actions are taken in these countries (Mansell & Wehn 1998).
In South Africa, it is quite commonly observed that access to ICTs is severely hampered by the lack of infrastructure, services and know-how. There is no denying that this analysis is correct, but only partly so. For instance, we know that South Africa's mobile infrastructure and coverage is very good. Given this observation, our conclusion can only be that affordability represents a significant constraint to access. This factor is at stake in the trend of fixed-line substitution in Sub-Saharan Africa (Esselaar and Stork 2005).

Of equal concern is the very marked urban–rural digital divide in South Africa. Rural areas not only lag behind in terms of ICT access, but also with regard to those factors (such as literacy, computer skills and higher household incomes) that could possibly contribute to the bridging of the urban–rural gap (Conradie, Morris & Jacobs 2003).

One of the major factors that has prevented many rural regions from benefiting fully from the potential of ICTs has been the low penetration and quality of fixed-line telecommunication services. Although recent developments and cost reductions in wireless communication technologies, including both local loop and satellite communications, permit the availability of telecommunication services at any spot on the globe, there is still a cost barrier that rural communities will not easily overcome. Furthermore, commercial service providers tend to concentrate rollout of infrastructure in metropolitan areas, where returns are less risky and where profitability is potentially higher.

This suggests the need for providing sustainable, cost-effective, shared-community ICT facilities, capable of servicing most of the requirements of the rural population. In recognition of this need, various public and private sector initiatives have been launched in South Africa to try and improve the telecommunications and electricity infrastructure across the country. Some initiatives have specifically incorporated elements of public access to telephony, computer literacy, Internet access and information provision in rural areas.

The international literature shows that while public access facilities have been given many names – telecentres, Multi-Purpose Community Centres, virtual village halls, electronic cottages, village knowledge centres, digital clubhouses, etc., – the word telecentre serves as a generic term to encompass this array of experiences (Gomez et al. 1999). Originating in Sweden around 1985, telecentres experienced fairly rapid growth in Western Europe and other industrialised countries where rural isolation, lack of purchasing power and low-quality telecommunications and information technology facilities were considered a hindrance to participation in the information economy (Oestmann & Dymond 2001).

In providing access to ICTs, telecentres are expected to have a positive impact on the socio-economic development of the communities they serve, helping to:
- Develop rural and remote infrastructure;
- Provide rural regions with better public services and improved local administration;
- Generate employment and foster socio-economic development;
- Integrate relatively isolated communities into the national and international information network and thus accelerate exchange of private goods and services;
- Transfer expertise to and from the community in a number of areas, such as agriculture; and
- Give local producers access to market information, thus reducing the need for middlemen and increasing rural incomes.

The South African government has identified a range of centres as community access points where ICT services are made available to the public on a full-time or part-time basis. The ICT service centres that will be discussed in the next sections, as implemented by government, include:
- Multi-Purpose Community Centres (MPCCs);
- Telecentres and Cyberlabs;
- Public Information Terminals (PITs); and
- Public libraries.

All these service centres have a particular profile of users. Consequently, in order to work towards achieving universal access, the managers and developers of these centres must consider what area they can cover or which community can be serviced within a certain distance from a particular service centre.

In order to calculate the population served by each public ICT service centre it was desirable to obtain data from each centre on the total number of people served over a unit period of time. These data were not available to the research team. As a result, the team opted to calculate the theoretical number of people that each centre could serve, based on the simple technique of creating a 5 km buffer zone around each centre. The population located within this 5 km zone was calculated as a measure of the theoretical number of clients who could be served. To achieve this, the distribution of the South African population was represented on the map as another layer.

In the following discussions on each type of centre, an estimate of the number of people who could access a centre is given. This number is calculated using GIS and consists of all people living within a 5 km of a centre. In some instances the number of people who live within the 5 km zone could not possibly be accommodated because the centre is located in a high population density area. On the other hand, other centres have a relatively small population to serve. This means that in the future, certain benchmarks regarding the number of people accommodated need to be devised. This will enable government to construct a clearer idea of how many people it can actually serve per centre in relation to the total number requiring service.

4.1 Multi-Purpose Community Centres (MPCC)

The Government Communication and Information System (GCIS) has been tasked to increase accessibility of government information and services and improve communication between the government and the people. The GCIS has identified the Multi-Purpose Community Centre (MPCC) as a primary vehicle for the implementation of developmental communication and information programmes. The MPCCs are intended to serve as a base from which a wide range of government services and products can reach communities. The aim is for communities to access such services and engage with government programmes for their own empowerment (GCIS 2001).

MPCCs are intended to be one-stop centres where local, provincial and national government, as well as other service providers, offer much-needed services and information about government programmes to local communities. Various forms of media, including print and electronic, as well as direct person-to-person communication with community members, are deployed to provide the required information. At least six government departments offering services to people in the locality are required to be represented at an MPCC. Each MPCC is unique and could either be located in a single building, or be part of a cluster of buildings (GCIS 2001).

GCIS works in partnership with the Universal Service and Access Agency of South Africa (USAASA) to rollout MPCCs. The role of USAASA is to set up a telecentre inside an existing MPCC as part of promoting access to technology and capacity building. In an MPCC, a telecentre provides services such as telephony, Internet, photocopying, scanning, faxing and computer training. The number of computers per telecentre located in an MPCC ranges from 10 to 25 (GCIS 2001).

4.1.1 Indicator 6: Access to Multi-Purpose Community Centres (MPCCs)

The distribution of MPCCs by province shows that there are currently 66 MPCCs in the country, with the majority in Gauteng (16). The lowest number of MPCCs per province is in the Eastern Cape, Free State and Northern Cape, each having 4 MPCCs (Table 4.1).

MPCCs are a responsibility of local governments and municipalities, with 48 of the 262 municipalities currently providing MPCC services. Given that there are 66 MPCCs in all, this means that some municipalities have more than one MPCC. A closer look at Table 4.1 shows that only 10 municipalities have more than 1 MPCC: City of Johannesburg (5), City of Cape Town (5), Ekurhuleni (4), Tshwane Metro (3), Randfontein (2), Mafube (2), Tubatse (2), Mangaung (2), George (2) and Sol Plaaitjie (2). Four of these municipalities are found in Gauteng while the Western Cape and Free State have two municipalities each. The municipalities with high population counts (over a million people), will theoretically need more MPCCs to be able to provide adequate ICT access. The analysis assumes that all MPCCs identified and located spatially are currently operating. However, it must be noted that the data supplied did not refer to the operational status of MPCCs, which may be in different stages of maturity.

Table 4.1: Distribution of population within 5 km radius of MPCC by province

Province	No. of municipalities	No. of municipalities with MPCC	No. of MPCCs in Province	Coverage: 5 km	Average coverage per MPCC
Eastern Cape	43	4	4	53 393	13 348
Free State	21	3	4	158 550	39 638
Gauteng	13	6	16	3 153 700	197 106
KwaZulu-Natal	55	6	6	71 284	11 881
Limpopo	23	7	9	133 416	14 824
Mpumalanga	24	5	5	124 958	24 992
North West	22	5	6	98 732	16 455
Northern Cape	31	4	4	227 045	56 761
Western Cape	30	8	12	2 111 690	175 974
Total	262	48	66	6 132 768	92 921

Source: GCIS 2005

The MPCCs serve an estimated total population of approximately 6 132 768 people (Table 4.1). This is based on a calculation of the number of people who reside within a 5 km radius of the MPCCs. The total population within a 5km radius of every MPCC in a province is divided by the number of MPCCs in order to create an average. This provides an indication of the potential demand for services per MPCC in each province (Table 4.1).

Gauteng, with its high population density, is the province with the highest number of MPCCs servicing a theoretical total population of 3 153 700 residing within a 5 km radius of the various MPCCs. This suggests that at this stage of the MPCC rollout programme, the population of Gauteng has relatively privileged access to MPCCs compared to other regions and provinces (see also Figure 4.1). However, high population density figures suggest that these MPCCs could easily be oversubscribed.

Figure 4.1: MPCCs showing serviced population within a 5 km radius

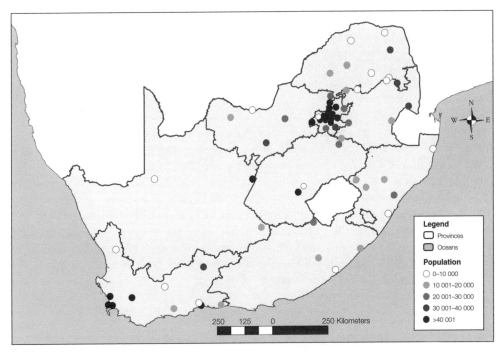

Source: GCIS 2005

The histogram in Figure 4.2 shows that the majority of MPCCs have an estimated resident adult population of between 10 000 and 40 000 within a 5 km radius that could require some form of communication service. A key issue in this regard is the kind of numbers that an MPCC could reasonably be expected to support.

Figure 4.2: Number of MPCCs servicing estimated population numbers within a 5 km radius

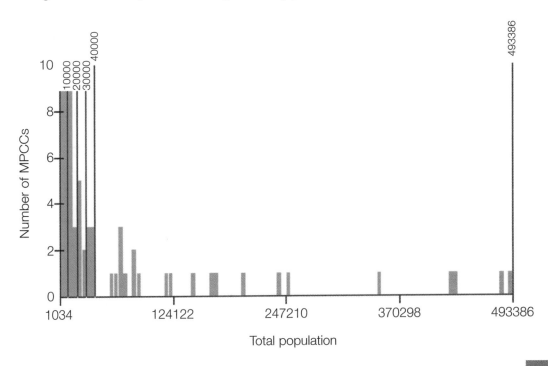

At the municipality level, Table 4.2 provides the name of the municipality, the number of MPCCs that it hosts and the combined total population residing within 5 km of all MPCCs in the municipality. The far-right column provides an average number of people that could theoretically expect service from an MPCC in that municipality. Where there is one MPCC, the population residing within 5 km is the same as the theoretical population demanding service. Thus, the theoretical population of 1 172 797 people that the five City of Johannesburg MPCCs serve means that each MPCC should, in theory, extend service provision to 29 199 people.

This exercise is presented to make several points. Firstly, the number of people theoretically expecting service from an MPCC varies substantially. The range extends from 293 199 for an MPCC in the City of Johannesburg to 1 837 for an MPCC at Setla-Kgobi Municipality. As a consequence, it will become important to monitor MPCCs in terms of how they provide and plan services for their immediate population. Consideration will also have to be given to the development of MPCCs graded according to size and capacity, in keeping with the population they are expected to serve. Benchmarks for these facilities, in terms of size and the nature and quality of service, will probably become necessary. These differences should not be ignored when addressing issues of how MPCCs provide for access to and use of ICTs.

Table 4.2: Distribution of population within 5 km radius of MPCC by municipality

Municipality	No. of MPCCs	Population coverage: 5 km	Average coverage per MPCC
City of Johannesburg	5	1 172 797	234 559
City of Cape Town	4	688 137	172 034
Ekurhuleni Metro	4	1 117 524	279 381
City of Tshwane	3	614 115	204 705
Randfontein	2	89 368	44 684
Mangaung	2	118 828	59 414
Tubatse	2	16 966	8 483
Sol Plaaitjie	2	209 609	104 805
Mafube	2	39 722	19 861
George	2	83 553	41 777
Emfuleni	1	27 631	27 631
Kungwini	1	23 669	23 669
Lesedi	1	39 417	39 417
Mutale	1	3 306	3 306
Mogalakwena	1	15 177	15 177
Blouberg	1	6 969	6 969
Modimolle	1	10 276	10 276

Access to information and telecommunications service centres

Municipality	No. of MPCCs	Population coverage: 5 km	Average coverage per MPCC
Giyani	1	37 865	37 865
Fetakgomo	1	7 393	7 393
Bushbuckridge	1	35 462	35 462
Port St Johns	1	11 895	11 895
Intsika Yethu	1	11 183	11 183
Mnquma	1	8 812	8 812
Senqu	1	21 503	21 503
Nkomazi	1	39 927	39 927
Govan Mbeki	1	22 130	22 130
Albert Luthuli	1	43 582	43 582
Dr JS Moroka	1	15 303	15 303
Greater Marble Hall	1	4 016	4 016
Moretele	1	23 965	23 965
Ventersdorp	1	98 974	98 974
Mamusa	1	32 813	32 813
Setla-Kgobi	1	1 837	1 837
Kagisano	1	12 170	12 170
Breede Valley	1	81 492	81 492
Matzikama	1	4 647	4 647
Plettenburg	1	15 542	15 542
Langeberg	1	12 544	12 544
Beaufort West	1	30 796	30 796
Laingsburg	1	4 399	4 399
Kai !Garib	1	2 809	2 809
Umsombovu	1	12 779	12 779
Ndwedwe	1	20 355	20 355
Umhlabauyalingana	1	6 225	6 225
Umsinga	1	12 629	12 629
Okhahlamba	1	12 022	12 022
Imbabazane	1	10 111	10 111
Vulamehlo	1	9 942	9 942

4.2 Telecentres and Cyberlabs

In an attempt to promote access to ICTs, the Telecommunications Act 103 of 1996 (South Africa 1996), as amended in 2001, mandated the USAASA to promote universal service and universal access in under-serviced areas of South Africa. To carry out this mandate the USAASA 'deploys telecentres and e-school Cyberlabs to deliver E-education, E-Business development of SMMEs and E-Government services in accordance with its corporate Plan' (USAASA 2004).

While there are various definitions of telecentres, a characteristic common to all is: a physical space that provides public access to ICTs for educational, personal, social, and economic development (Gomez et al. 1999). Telecentres are communication access points deployed in needy areas with no access or low levels of telecommunications access. The main purpose of telecentres is to provide information and communications services in order to bridge the digital divide.

Telecentres have diverse ownership structures: individuals, non-governmental organisations (NGOs), community-based organisations (CBOs) and small medium and micro enterprises (SMMEs). Although the equipment available in each centre differs, most telecentres provide computer services, voice (telephones), data (Internet and email), video (DVD and CD-ROM), typing, fax, printing and photocopying facilities, as well as computer literacy skills training (USAASA 2004).

The USAASA is directed to deploy e-School Cyberlabs in under-serviced areas, particularly rural, peri-urban and underdeveloped townships. e-School Cyberlabs are school-based facilities where science teachers are trained in basic computing. Cyberlabs are limited to the school community and provide ICT services and computer literacy training. The training programme focuses on the following four areas:
- Promoting human resources development in ICT software;
- Providing a managed facility that enables students to understand and learn to utilise the Internet and related network and software technologies;
- Educating students in the use of opportunities presented by the Internet; and
- Providing universal access for students under controlled circumstances and in a regulated environment.

Each Cyberlab is supposed to have about 30 computers and one each of a photocopying machine, printer and fax machine, where there is a need. The USAASA is responsible for the installation of network points, air-conditioners and the provision of security for the facility. Each school is supposed to own its Cyberlab and to be responsible for all maintenance costs, except Internet connectivity. Internet costs are provided for by the USAASA for a period of 12 months, thereafter the school becomes fully responsible for the Cyberlab.

Through a partnership with Digital Partnership, the USAASA is currently rolling out refurbished computers to schools in disadvantaged areas of South Africa (USAASA 2004).

4.2.1 Indicator 7: Access to telecentres

There are 103 telecentres, with three or more located in each of the nine provinces. The total population resident within 5 km of every telecentre that theoretically could expect to be serviced is 5 458 073. This represents an average theoretical client base of 52 991 per telecentre (Table 4.3).

At the provincial level, Limpopo (30) and KwaZulu-Natal (19) have more telecentres compared to the other provinces, which have between 3 and 12 telecentres. Relative to other provinces, Limpopo and KwaZulu-Natal have a greater relative share of telecentres, a situation warranted by the fact that they also have a substantial number of under-serviced rural areas that lack access to ICT services.

Table 4.3: Distribution of population within 5 km radius of telecentres by province

Province	No. of municipalities	No. of municipalities with telecentre	No. of telecentres in municipalities	Coverage: 5 km	Average coverage per telecentre
Eastern Cape	43	9	12	277 769	23 147
Free State	21	5	7	156 309	22 330
Gauteng	13	7	13	2 509 636	193 049
KwaZulu-Natal	55	17	19	827 952	43 576
Mpumalanga	24	5	6	82 446	13 741
Limpopo	23	17	30	476 155	15 872
North West	22	7	7	186 882	26 697
Northern Cape	31	3	3	13 611	4 537
Western Cape	30	3	6	927 313	154 552
Total	262	73	103	5 458 073	52 991

Source: USAASA 2005

The 103 telecentres are found in 73 municipalities. Only 18 of the 73 municipalities have more than one telecentre. Polokwane municipality has the highest number of telecentres (5), while the municipalities with the lowest number of telecentres are found in the Northern Cape and Western Cape, each having 3 telecentres (Figure 4.3).

Figure 4.3: Telecentres showing serviced population within a 5 km radius

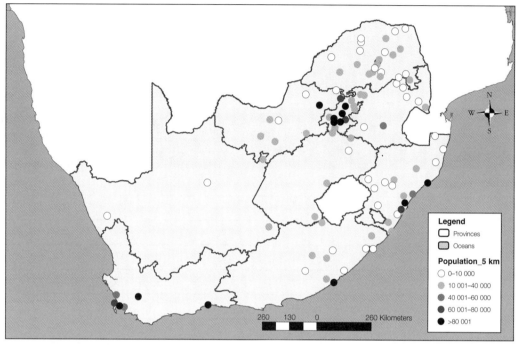

Source: USAASA 2005

The histogram in Figure 4.4 reveals that the majority of telecentres are estimated to have a potential resident adult population of between 10 000 and 40 000 to service within a 5 km radius.

Figure 4.4: Number of telecentres servicing estimated population numbers within a 5 km radius

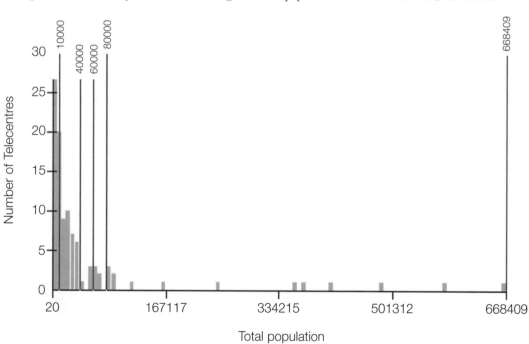

At the municipal level, Table 4.4 provides the name of the municipality, the number of telecentres that it hosts and the combined total population residing within 5 km of all telecentres in the municipality. The far-right column provides an estimate of the average number of people who could theoretically expect service from a telecentre in that municipality. Where there is one telecentre, the population residing within 5 km is the same as the theoretical population demanding service. Thus, the theoretical population of 126 494 people that the five Polokwane Municipality telecentres serve means that each telecentre should, in theory, extend service provision to 25 299 people.

The number of people theoretically expecting service from a telecentre varies substantially. The range extends from 374 677 for a telecentre in the City of Johannesburg to 20 for a telecentre in Bo Karoo Municipality. This analysis shows that despite the number of centres available, municipalities with high population densities may be expected to provide access to ICT services to substantial numbers of people, thus raising issues relating to the quality and availability of services. As a consequence it will become important to grade telecentres according to size and capacity in accordance with the population they are expected to serve. Benchmarks for these facilities, in terms of size and the nature and quality of service, will probably become necessary.

Table 4.4: Distribution of population within a 5 km radius of a telecentre by municipality

Municipality	No. of telecentres	Total population within 5 km	Average coverage per telecentre
Polokwane	5	126 494	25 299
City of Cape Town	4	763 390	190 848
Blouberg	4	13 393	3 348
Ekurhuleni Metro	4	1 315 834	328 959
Ethekwini Metro	3	551 958	183 986
Port St Johns	3	8 446	2 815
Buffalo City	2	174 531	87 266
City of Johannesburg	2	749 354	374 677
Kungwini	2	49 331	24 666
City of Tshwane	2	312 637	156 319
Nkomazi	2	24 802	12 401
Mutale	2	5 153	2 577
Greater Groblersdal	2	47 469	23 735
Fetakgomo	2	23 663	11 832
Greater Tubatse	2	9 687	4 844
Lepele-Nkumpi	2	35 086	17 543
Makhado	2	66 742	33 371
Greater Letaba	2	22 146	11 073

Municipality	No. of telecentres	Total population within 5 km	Average coverage per telecentre
Modimolle	1	10 276	10 276
Greater Giyani	1	37 865	37 865
Bushbuckridge	1	39 873	39 873
Maruleng	1	2 287	2 287
Mogalakwena	1	15 179	15 179
Phokwane	1	18 103	18 103
Lephalale	1	2 739	2 739
Umshwathi	1	20 355	20 355
Okhahlamba	1	1 687	1 687
Vulamehlo	1	9 942	9 942
Ingwe	1	4 974	4 974
The Big 5 False Bay	1	2 450	2 450
Hibiscus Coast	1	12 695	12 695
Umzumbe	1	12 068	12 068
Umhlabuyalingana	1	6 225	6 225
KwaDukuza	1	57 897	57 897
Msinga	1	12 629	12 629
Jozini	1	6 440	6 440
Imbabazane	1	2 560	2 560
Umvoti	1	2 701	2 701
Ulundi	1	27 579	27 579
Umhlathuze	1	90 525	90 525
Umtshezi	1	5 267	5 267
Nokeng tsa Taemane	1	21 022	21 022
Randfontein	1	33 827	33 827
Emfuleni	1	27 631	27 631
Msukaligwa	1	43 582	43 582
Thaba Chweu	1	2 876	2 876
Highveld East	1	1 966	1 966
Mbombela	1	9 220	9 220
Lukanji	1	28 555	28 555
Qaukeni	1	17 603	17 603

ACCESS TO INFORMATION AND TELECOMMUNICATIONS SERVICE CENTRES

Municipality	No. of telecentres	Total population within 5 km	Average coverage per telecentre
Nkonkobe	1	3 234	3 234
Mnquma	1	8 812	8 812
Intsika Yethu	1	11 183	11 183
Senqu	1	21 503	21 503
Engcobo	1	3 902	3 902
George	1	82 431	82 431
Breede Valley	1	81 492	81 492
Moretele	1	8 830	8 830
City Council of Klerksdorp	1	36 821	36 821
Moses Kotane	1	3 242	3 242
Rustenburg	1	90 096	90 096
Mamusa	1	32 696	32 696
Setla-Kgobi	1	12 944	12 944
Mafikeng	1	2 253	2 253
Bo Karoo	1	20	20
Umsombomvu	1	12 778	12 778
Kamiesberg	1	813	813

4.2.2 Indicator 8: Access to Cyberlabs

The majority of Cyberlabs are found in schools in KwaZulu Natal (38), the Eastern Cape (34) and Limpopo (30), compared to 7 in Gauteng and 3 in the Western Cape (Table 4.5). This is mainly in line with the mandate of the USAASA to establish these Internet laboratories in rural, peri-urban and under-serviced areas.

Table 4.5: Distribution of secondary school aged population within a 5 km radius of a Cyberlab by province

Province	No. of municipalities	No. of municipalities with Cyberlabs	No. of Cyberlabs in municipalities	Total population aged 15–19 years within 5 km	Average coverage per Cyberlab
Eastern Cape	43	18	34	105 179	3 094
Free State	21	10	14	24 516	1 751
Gauteng	13	4	7	74 294	10 613
KwaZulu-Natal	55	26	38	217 848	5 733
Limpopo	23	15	30	107 727	3 591
Mpumalanga	24	10	24	59 086	2 462
North West	22	5	10	17 680	1 768
Northern Cape	31	11	26	48 165	1 853
Western Cape	30	2	3	86 457	28 819
Total	262	101	186	740 952	3 984

Source: USAASA 2005

This pattern is naturally visible at the municipal level, where there are 26 municipalities in KwaZulu-Natal, 18 in the Eastern Cape and 15 in Limpopo that have Cyberlabs (Table 4.5). The municipalities with the most Cyberlabs, Ga Segonyane (8) and Thaba Chweu (8) are found in the Northern Cape and Mpumalanga respectively (Table 4.6).

Table 4.5 also shows that an estimated 740 952 young people of secondary-school age – aged 15 to 19 years – are resident within 5 km of a Cyberlab (see also Figure 4.5). This is not to suggest that primary school learners are not serviced by Cyberlabs. The calculation is made in order to show the potential school-aged population that could access a Cyberlab in their locality. The provinces best served by Cyberlabs combine a higher numbers of labs with a lower average number of would-be clients within a range of labs. The provinces with the lowest Cyberlab service are Western Cape and Gauteng, two provinces that are best serviced in almost all other aspects of private and public ICT access. Clearly, Cyberlabs have been appropriately placed in provinces where there is greater need for government-supported ICT provision. However, the average client populations for KwaZulu-Natal are relatively high, which suggests that even within the range of currently existing Cyberlabs, a case could be made for the placement of more such facilities. The development of norms for such resource allocation decisions will be important.

ACCESS TO INFORMATION AND TELECOMMUNICATIONS SERVICE CENTRES

Figure 4.5: Cyberlabs showing serviced secondary school aged population within a 5 km radius

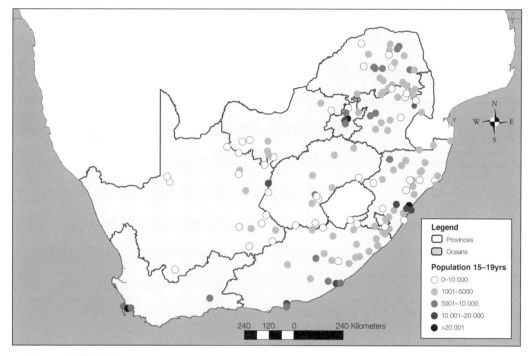

Source: USAASA 2005

At the municipal level, Table 4.6 provides the name of the municipality, the number of Cyberlabs that it hosts and the combined total school-aged population aged 15–19 years that resides within 5 km of all Cyberlabs in the municipality. The far-right column provides an average number of school-aged learners aged 15–19 years that could theoretically expect service from a Cyberlab in that municipality. Where there is one Cyberlab, the school-aged population residing within 5 km is the same as the theoretical population demanding service. Thus, the theoretical population of 10 789 school-aged learners that the 8 Cyberlabs in Thaba Chweu Municipality serve means that each Cyberlab should, in theory, extend service provision to 1 349 learners.

Table 4.6: Distribution of secondary school aged population within a 5 km radius of a Cyberlab by municipality

Municipality	No. of Cyberlabs	Population aged 15–19 years within 5 km	Average coverage per Cyberlab
Ga-Segonyana	8	7 630	954
Thaba Chweu	8	10 789	1 349
Ethekwini Metro	6	144 104	24 017
Intsika Yethu	5	5 528	1 106
Mangaung	5	12 273	2 455
Mbombela	5	17 710	3 542
Greater Taung	4	6 488	1 622

Municipality	No. of Cyberlabs	Population aged 15–19 years within 5 km	Average coverage per Cyberlab
Greater Tubatse	4	4 123	1 031
Makhado	4	12 654	3 164
Umzimkhulu	2	3 618	1 809
Buffalo City	3	27 247	9 082
City of Cape Town	3	80 418	26 806
Emalahleni	3	8 218	2 739
Kgatelopele	3	1 594	531
Makhuduthamaga	3	7 785	2 595
Mbizana	2	4 291	2 146
Naledi	3	8 799	2 933
Polokwane	3	22 000	7 333
Sol Plaaitjie	3	30 018	10 006
Thulamela	3	27 524	9 175
Ulundi	3	7 040	2 347
Abaqulusi	2	9 030	4 515
Albert Luthuli	2	2 121	1 061
Ba-Phalaborwa	2	7 613	3 807
Blouberg	2	2 469	1 235
Bushbuckridge	2	6 027	3 014
City of Tshwane	2	8 424	4 212
Ekurhuleni Metro	2	44 214	22 107
Emthanjeni	2	3 432	1 716
Greater Giyani	2	8 758	4 379
Greater Tzaneen	2	1 918	959
Kai! Garib	2	252	126
King Sabata Dalindyebo	2	3 318	1 659
Kungwini	2	4 444	2 222
Mbonambi	2	2 658	1 329
Middelburg	2	8 880	4 440
Moshaweng	2	762	381
Nelson Mandela	2	26 546	13 273
Nkandla	2	2 663	1 332

Access to information and telecommunications service centres

Municipality	No. of Cyberlabs	Population aged 15–19 years within 5 km	Average coverage per Cyberlab
Qaukeni	2	6 384	3 192
Renosterberg	2	649	325
Senqu	2	2 153	1 077
Ubuhlebezwe	2	2 674	1 337
Ubuntu	2	431	216
Umsombomvu	2	2 287	1 144
uMuziwabantu	2	2 080	1 040
Umzimvubu	2	1 440	720
Aganang	1	821	821
City of Johannesburg	1	17 210	17 210
Dr JS Moroka	1	1 117	1 117
Elundini	1	1 965	1 965
Emnambithi/Ladysmith	1	4 347	4 347
Endumeni	1	3 086	3 086
Fetakgomo	1	1 804	1 804
Greater Groblersdal	1	2 091	2 091
Greater Kokstad	1	3 476	3 476
Greater Letaba	1	3 544	3 544
Highveld East	1	3 210	3 210
Ingwe	1	762	762
Inxuba Yethemba	1	3 561	3 561
Jozini	1	1 206	1 206
Kalahari	1	105	105
Karoo Hoogland	1	154	154
Kopanong	1	821	821
Lepele-Nkumpi	1	3 236	3 236
Letsemeng	1	728	728
Lukanji	1	6 404	6 404
Mafube	1	2 888	2 888
Maletswai	1	3 665	3 665
Maluti a Phofung	1	41	41
Maphumulo	1	1 763	1 763

Municipality	No. of Cyberlabs	Population aged 15–19 years within 5 km	Average coverage per Cyberlab
Masilonyana	1	2 461	2 461
Mbhashe	1	2 177	2 177
Mhlontlo	1	1 401	1 401
Mohokare	1	898	898
Moses Kotane	1	2 027	2 027
Msukaligwa	1	4 762	4 762
Msunduzi	1	10 124	10 124
Mthonjaneni	1	736	736
Mtubatuba	1	2 455	2 455
Newcastle	1	7 731	7 731
Ngwathe	1	1 009	1 009
Nkomazi	1	2 668	2 668
Nkonkobe	1	3 092	3 092
Nongoma	1	2 182	2 182
Nqutu	1	1 761	1 761
Nyandeni	1	1 138	1 138
Okhahlamba	1	133	133
Oudtshoorn	1	6 035	6 035
Richmond	1	2 502	2 502
Rustenburg	1	786	786
Setsoto	1	2 217	2 217
Siyancuma	1	1 617	1 617
Umdoni	1	985	985
Umhlabuyalingana	1	1 495	1 495
uMlalazi	1	1 242	1 242
Umvoti	1	179	179
uPhongolo	1	1 746	1 746
Total	186	745 042	4 006

The histogram in Figure 4.6 shows that the majority of Cyberlabs service a secondary school aged population (15–19 years) of 1 000 to 5 000 people within a 5 km radius. About 16 Cyberlabs are located in areas where the potential client population aged 15–19 years is greater than 10 000.

Figure 4.6: Number of Cyberlabs showing secondary school aged population serviced within a 5 km radius

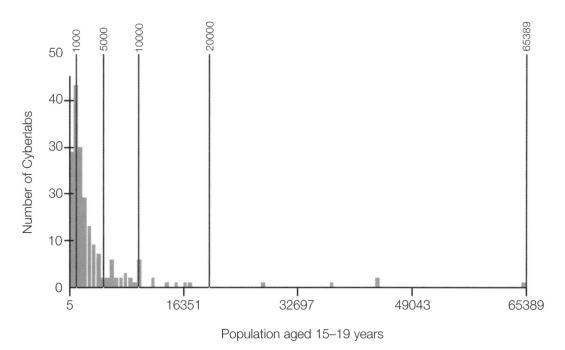

As indicated for MPCCs and telecentres, the number of people (aged 15–19) theoretically expecting service from a Cyberlab varies substantially. This range extends from an average of 26 806 people having access to a Cyberlab in the City of Cape Town to an average of 41 people having access to a Cyberlab in Maluti a Phofung. As a consequence it will become important to grade Cyberlabs according to size and capacity and to benchmark facilities in accordance with the population they are expected to serve.

4.3 Public Information Terminals

Launched in 1998 as a joint project between the Department of Communications and the South African Post Office, Public Information Terminals (PITs) represent a new way of bridging the digital divide. PITs are multimedia kiosks designed to provide two-way communication services. These kiosks are located in post offices and other access sites, such as MPCCs, to give communities access to the following services, although these might vary among PITs:
- Government services to provide access to government information
  (i.e. government forms, news, jobs, etc.);
- Internet services to allow users to get information on any topic of their choice;
- Email to give users access to create their own email account;
- Business services to give users the opportunity to select goods and services from the businesses that advertise; and
- Educational services to give users access to information on various courses from different institutions and even the opportunity of applying online.

4.3.1 Indicator 9: Access to Public Information Terminals (PITs)

In analysing the data on Public Information Terminals, one has to consider the unequal distribution of postal services that prevailed under the previous dispensation. Many areas, especially rural areas, are still without a post office, making it difficult to connect the PITs to telephone lines and the Internet. However, in those areas with infrastructure, the data show that while some post offices currently have PITs that are connected, a number of these multimedia kiosks are not yet online – although this is planned for the near future. Of the 698 PITs available in the various post offices throughout the country, 353 are already operating and another 345 have yet to come online. The majority of those that are online are found in KwaZulu-Natal (54) while the smallest number online (22) is in the Northern Cape.

At the provincial level, Table 4.7 provides information on the population resident within a 5 km radius of a stated number of operational and not yet online PITs. The far-right column provides an average number of people that could in theory expect service from an operational PIT in that province.

As indicated for MPCCs, telecentres and Cyberlabs, the number of people theoretically expecting service from a PIT varies substantially. In Gauteng, the average population coverage of a PIT is 142 049 people whereas it is 18 730 in Mpumalanga. The implications of this information for service quality, accessibility, maintenance and costs to the post office can only be mentioned here as a matter for further research.

Table 4.7: Distribution of population within a 5 km radius of a PIT by province

Province	No. of PITS	No. not online	No. online	Total population per 5 km	Average coverage per PIT
Eastern Cape	94	63	31	1 918 024	61 872
Free State	74	30	44	1 563 696	35 539
Gauteng	78	32	46	6 534 262	142 049
KwaZulu-Natal	80	26	54	4 476 379	82 896
Limpopo	91	57	34	651 844	19 172
Mpumalanga	75	40	35	655 548	18 730
North West	84	41	43	1 522 354	35 404
Northern Cape	52	30	22	866 449	39 384
Western Cape	70	26	44	5 250 910	119 339
Total	698	345	353	23 439 466	66 401

The histogram in Figure 4.7 shows the distribution of PITs according to the total estimated population they are expected to serve. The majority of PITs have between 50 000 and 100 000 people within a 5 km radius – a seemingly large number of potential users. Naturally, all people within range of a PIT would not necessarily want to make use of its facilities with equal frequency. There is a need to investigate PIT usage patterns to get a sense of how intensively they are used and whether these PITs are meeting the needs of users, depending on the community in which they are located.

Figure 4.7: Number of PITs showing serviced population within a 5 km radius

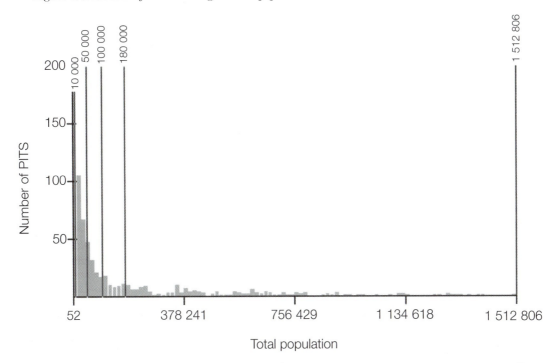

4.4 Libraries

As has been observed, the creation and use of an indicator is dictated by the extent to which that indicator is useful for monitoring and decision-making in a specific national context. In a developing country like South Africa, the decision was made to include libraries in this set of ICT indicators, as explained below.

Firstly, by definition ICTs are a means of information sourcing and manipulation, and communication. Where the general level of access to ICT is still growing, it is important to factor in institutions such as libraries, which have traditionally served and still serve as information sources.

Secondly, many of the information-management skills that are particularly necessary in a digital environment can be learned using books and other sources of printed matter.

Thirdly, unlocking the information and opportunities of the Internet demands a certain degree of reading ability. Although reading is generally recognised as a fundamental requirement for personal development, international indexes reveal that reading literacy scores are very low in many countries. Libraries serve not only as sources of information in their own right, but also as places where the essential skill of literacy can be learned and practised.

Fourthly, libraries are seen as logical places where ICT facilities can be deployed, as they are often well placed for access by members of the community. Increasingly, libraries are offering access to digital resources, such as online catalogues and general information via the Internet.

4.4.1 Indicator 10: Access to libraries

As public institutions, public libraries continue to serve as important sources of information for many South Africans in both rural and urban areas. There are currently 1 242 public libraries throughout the country. The majority of these libraries are found in the Western Cape (237), followed by Gauteng (215). Limpopo has only 32 public libraries.

Table 4.8 shows that 198 of the 262 municipalities in the country have public libraries. With the exception of KwaZulu-Natal, more than half of the municipalities in each province offer library services to the public. In some instances, the figure is much higher; for example, of the 21 municipalities in the Free State, 19 have public libraries and in Mpumalanga, 21 out of 23 municipalities have public libraries.

Table 4.8: Distribution of public libraries by province

Province	No. of municipalities	No. of municipalities with libraries	No. of libraries
Eastern Cape	43	34	141
Free State	21	19	136
Gauteng	13	12	215
KwaZulu-Natal	55	24	205
Limpopo	24	15	32
Mpumalanga	23	21	90
Northern Cape	31	27	101
North West	31	21	85
Western Cape	30	25	237
Total	262	198	1 242

Source: National Library of South Africa 2005

CHAPTER 5

Under-serviced areas

5.1 Under-Serviced Area Licences

In South Africa, there are areas that are under-serviced in terms of access to telecommunications. These are most commonly areas that have not been considered commercially viable by the fixed-line and cellphone providers on account of low-population densities, low-income communities (who would struggle to pay for the service) and the costs of implementing a service infrastructure. In many instances these areas are rural, comprising isolated communities of historically disadvantaged people. In response to this undesirable situation, Under-Serviced Area Licenses (USALs) were developed to meet the communication needs of these communities.

The Telecommunications Amendment Act (2001) provides for USALs to be issued to small, medium and micro-enterprises (SMMEs) and co-operatives to supply telecommunication services. The aim is to lower telephone costs in rural areas and for low-income clients, as well as to provide discounts to schools, health facilities, libraries and other developmental institutions so that telephone services and connectivity to the Internet can be sustained.

SMMEs are licensed to provide local-loop public-switched telecommunications services, which include fixed, mobile and public pay phones and Voice Over Internet Protocol (VOIP). These services should be available to areas where less than 5 per cent of the local population has access to telecommunications (i.e. where teledensity is less than 5 per cent). The SMMEs are expected to use their own or leased infrastructure to enable them to connect to current telecommunications operator networks. As part of the license agreements, these SMMEs will receive a subsidy from the Universal Service and Access Agency of South Africa (USAASA).

The 27 designated USAL licence areas potentially cover 21.4 million people, representing 45 per cent of the population (ICT World 2005).

5.1.1 Indicator 11: Location and operation of Under-Serviced Area Licenses

In 2003, the telecommunications regulator, ICASA, received 16 submissions as part of Phase One of the USAL licensing process in the following provinces and municipalities: Limpopo (Capricorn Municipality), KwaZulu-Natal (Ugu and Zululand Municipalities), Eastern Cape (Tambo and Amatole Municipalities), Free State (Northern Free State and Lejweleputswa), North West (Central and Bophirima) (Sithole 2004).

In the 2004/05 financial year, the USAASA signed agreements with the first four USAL licensees for the following district municipalities and provinces: Capricorn in Limpopo, Ugu and Zululand in KwaZulu-Natal and Tambo in the Eastern Cape. In 2005, the Ministry of Communications announced that Phase Two of the USAL licensing process for an additional 14 areas was open for the submission of bids.

Figure 5.1 shows seven USAL licences located in the provinces of the Free State, KwaZulu-Natal, North West and Limpopo, which in 2005 provided services to 39 municipalities.

Figure 5.1: Under-Serviced Area Licences by district municipality

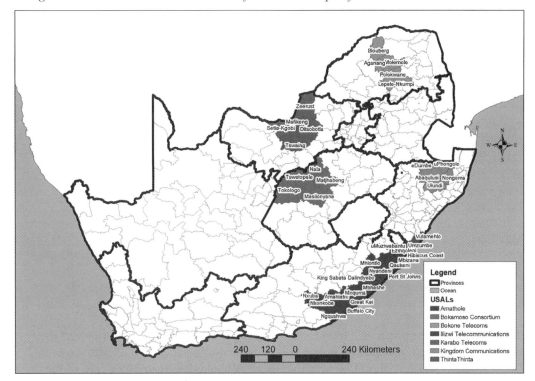

Source: USAASA 2005

5.1.2 USAL indicator development

As shown in Figure 5.1, Indicator 11 presents the spatial coverage of USALs. At this stage, it is a very simple indicator of coverage by USALs. As the USAL implementation rolls out, we may represent USAL coverage as a proportion of areas that are known to have access levels below particular benchmarks.

It will also be important to undertake further analysis of the impact of USAL service provision. USALs may have different impacts depending on the existing coverage. For instance, Mafikeng is an area with high mobile coverage, but very low Internet access – will USALs exert a different influence on usage patterns in other areas with typically low fixed line coverage?

CHAPTER 6

Composite indicators of access to ICT

6.1 Development of composite indicators

Based on 9 of the previous 11 indicators, 2 composite indicators were developed to capture the overall state of ICT access across the country. The indicators were developed in order to present two dimensions of ICT access: private access and public provision. The assumption was that public provision should, where possible, improve ICT access in areas where private service provision has not yet achieved desirable levels of access and quality.

The composite indicator on private ICT access was developed from the following variables: access to landline telephones (number of households with access to main telephone lines), number of households with access to cellular telephones, access to computers (number of households with access to personal computers), and access to the Internet (number of households with Internet access).

The composite indicator on public ICT access included variables that described public access to the different kinds of information and telecommunication service centres (e.g. access to MPCCs, telecentres, Cyberlabs, libraries and PITs).

The private ICT access composite indicator is based on data at the magisterial area level. As a result, the sub-indicators could be calculated on the basis of access per 1 000 households in each municipality. This could not be done for the public ICT access indicators. This is because the data available provided only the actual location of each facility. This is therefore point-source data and cannot be simply related to area-based data such as population. For this reason, the results from the composite indicator of private access were not combined with the results of the composite indicator of public access to create a single indicator.

6.2 Composite indicator 1: Private access (Indicator 12)

This composite indicator was calculated using the following formula with variables from the modelled SASAS survey:

Composite Private ICT access indicator = (% Households with access to landlines + % Households with access to mobile phones + % Households with access to PCs + % Households with access to Internet) ÷ 4

Therefore, the value obtained for each municipality is an unweighted average of the four area-based indicators used separately in this report as Indicators 1, 2, 4 and 5.

As shown in the histogram in Figure 6.1, in this composite index most of the municipalities are concentrated between 6.50 and 17.55. In real terms, when a municipality has a rating of 10.00 this means that on average only one in ten households has access to a landline, a mobile phone, a computer and the Internet. The graphic also shows that in only 13 municipalities are at least one in four households able to access all four items. As can be seen from this distribution, there are about 14 municipalities that visibly fall below the

6.5 level. This group can be targeted immediately on the basis of their low averages (the national average was 14.3.).

Figure 6.1: Number of municipalities according to private access to ICT indicator

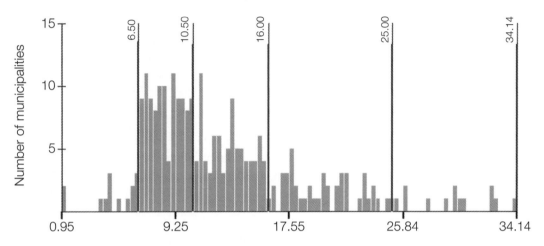

Despite the improvements in access to voice telephony made possible by cellphones, most people in South Africa have low levels of access to ICTs (in areas with maximum ICT access, not more than 42.64 per cent of households have access, as shown on Figure 6.2.) Referring to Figure 6.2, areas with the highest access (the dark charcoal areas on the map) show only 28.51 to 42.64 per cent of households having access to ICTs. In the areas with the least access (coloured light grey), only 0.24 to 6.15 per cent of households have access to ICTs. The map reveals that the gap in ICT access is primarily between the urban centres and the rural periphery. The digital divide is especially visible between the metropolitan areas and the rest of the country.

Areas with the highest combined private ICT access (28.51 to 42.64) include:
- The City of Cape Town;
- Nelson Mandela Metropole and Buffalo City in the Eastern Cape;
- eThekwini Metropole and Hibuscus Coast in KwaZulu-Natal;
- Mangaung Metropole, Kopanong, Matjhabeng and Ngwathe municipalities in the Free State;
- Klerksdorp and Rustenburg municipalities in the North West;
- City of Johannesburg and City of Tshwane in Gauteng;
- Middelburg, Mbombela and Thaba Cheu municipalities in Mpumalanga; and
- Polokwane and Makhado municipalities in Limpopo.

Areas with low access (0.24 to 6.15) with access to private ICTs include:
- Benede Oranje, Namaqualand and Diamondfields municipalities in the Northern Cape;
- Molopo Municipality in the North West;
- uMkhanyakunde, uMgungundlovu, and Sisonke municipalities and Giant's Castle Reserve in KwaZulu-Natal; and
- a small area in Gauteng that predominantly consists of nature reserves (the Hartebeeshoek, Johan Ness and Rhino and Lion nature reserves).

Figure 6.2: Indicator of private ICT access in South Africa per municipality

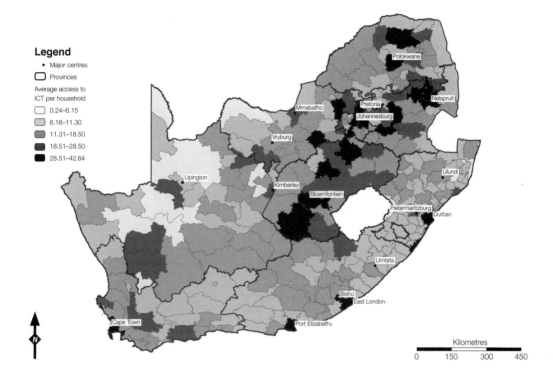

6.3 Composite indicator 2: Public access (Indicator 13)

As discussed earlier, the majority of people in developing countries gain access to ICTs through public facilities developed by government agencies. This makes measuring public access to community ICT facilities particularly important. Consequently, an indicator of public access involves measuring the number of public localities capable of providing access to ICT services to the population in a particular area, such as a municipality.

In this research report, the following four indicators were identified to capture the overall state of access to public information and telecommunication service centres across the country: Multi-Purpose Community Centres (MPCCs), telecentres and Cyberlabs, libraries, and Public Information Terminals (PITs).

The technique for estimating the population served by public ICT access centres has been explained earlier, when the report considered individual indicators. The team opted to calculate the theoretical number of people that each centre could serve based on the simple technique of creating 5 km buffer zones around each centre. For example, the population located inside of a 5 km range from a centre was calculated as a measure of the theoretical number of clients who could be served.

However, in the case of the composite public indicator, a different calculation was utilised. A composite indicator for access to public ICT service centres was calculated using the following formula per municipality: (N of MPCC + N of PIT + N of Cyberlabs + N of telecentres + N of libraries / total population per municipality in 2005) × 1 000.

Put more simply this means:

$$\text{Composite index per municipality} = \frac{\text{total number of centres}}{\text{total population}} \times 1000$$

This calculation provides a ratio of existing ICT services per 1 000 of the population. Such a calculation makes it possible to compare municipalities with different population sizes and different numbers of public ICT service centres. (The national average was 0.1.)

As shown in the histogram in Figure 6.3, the overwhelming majority of municipalities have less than 2 public ICT service centres per 1 000 people. A large number of municipalities – more than 40 – have from zero public ICT service centres to one centre per 1 000 people.

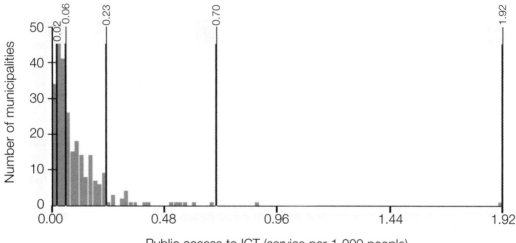

Figure 6.3: Number of municipalities according to public access to ICT indicator

Figure 6.4 shows that there is a distinct variance across provinces and municipalities in the distribution of ICT service centres. Most municipalities fall in the range of 0.07–0.23. These are spread across all nine provinces, but the majority (21) are in the Western Cape. The highest number of ICT services per 1 000 people is in the range of 0.71–1.92. Only two municipalities fall in this range: the Kalahari municipality in the Northern Cape (0.89) and the Lowveld municipality in Mpumalanga (1.92). However, these are small municipalities providing access to 6 834 and 520 people, respectively. These two municipalities therefore seem to be outliers in the data and do not represent the average situation. Interestingly, there are some instances of very high differences in the number of ICT outlets between adjacent municipalities. The map depicts the Northern Cape as a case in point. The differences in access to public ICT centres within each province are symptomatic of inequality in terms of ICT service provision.

The municipalities with the second highest number of access to public ICTs (0.24–0.70) are in the Northern Cape. There are 15 municipalities in this range: Richtersveld, Kamiesberg, Hantam, Karoo Hoogland, Khai-Ma, Ubuntu, Umsombovu, Kareeberg, Renosterberg, Thembelihle, Siyathemba, Siyancuma, Mier, Kgatelopele, Bo-Karoo. All these municipalities provide access to ICT service centres to a population of less than 40000. However, this high access ranking must be understood in the context of dispersed populations and large land areas in these municipalities. Other municipalities in this range are Swellendam and Langeberg (Western Cape), Kruger Park (Mpumalanga), Maletswai

(Eastern Cape) and Kopanong and Mohokare (Free State). Another observation must be that the majority of municipalities offer PITs and library services only.

At the lower end of public access to ICT service centres are those municipalities falling in the range of 0.00 to 0.02 per 1 000 people. There are 20 municipalities with no existing ICT service centres, although many of these are nature reserves. Other municipalities in this category are those that are highly populated but with few ICT services centres. The majority of these municipalities are found in the Eastern Cape and KwaZulu-Natal, and include:
- Umzimkulu, Umzimvubu, Amahlati, Mnquma, Mbhashe, Ngqushwa, Engcobo, Sakhisizwe, Mbizana, Qaukeni, NtabankuluNyandeni, Mhlontlo, King Sabata Dalindyebo;
- Umzumbe, Ezinqoleni, Umsunduzi, Imbabazane, Msinga, Dannhauser, eDumbe, Uphongolo, Nongoma, Endondakusuka, Ndwedwe, Maphumulo;
- Dr JS Moroka in Mpumalanga;
- Mutale, Thulamela in Limpopo;
- Moshaweng in North West; and
- Phokwane in Northern Cape.

The composite indicator on public access to ICTs shows that high concentrations of ICT service centres are largely found in urban municipalities, as compared to the low levels found in largely rural municipalities. These differences illustrate the unequal distribution of public ICT service between urban and rural areas.

Figure 6.4: Indicator of public access to ICT in South Africa per municipality

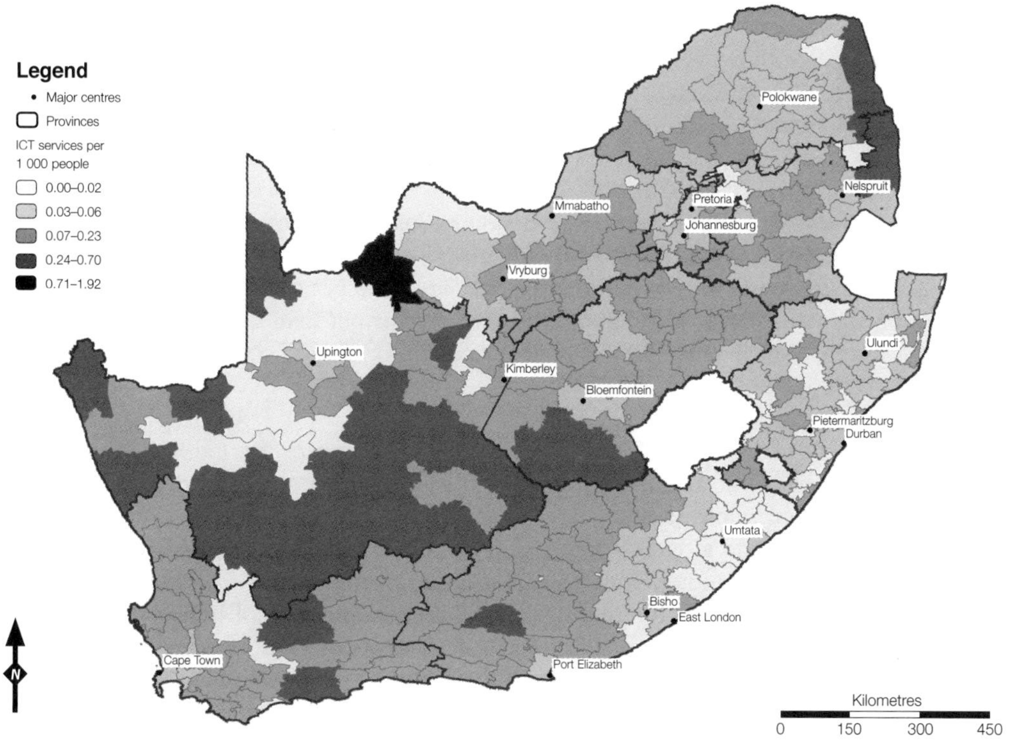

Source: HSRC 2005

CHAPTER 7

Conclusions and recommendations

7.1 Conclusions

The South African telecommunications sector has made significant progress in the provision of ICT over the last decade. However, social and economic divides still prevail. This led to delegates at the Gauteng Intergovernmental Infrastructure Summit to argue that the gap between the first and the second economies has to be closed by providing access to ICTs (Canada High Commission Trade Office 2005). Areas with poor ICT availability are likely to be considered less favourable for economic investment, thereby limiting enterprise development, job creation and restricting the growth of SMMEs, which are currently seen as a key driver of economic growth (Jacobs and Herselman 2005).

ICT penetration in both household and public sectors varies between and within provinces, creating a digital divide between those with high and those with low access levels. The gap in ICT access between metropoles, urban areas and rural areas could exacerbate existing inequalities and social problems. Effective deployment of ICTs may enable the country to accelerate the economic growth rate, on the basis of the potential of ICTs to increase efficiency and productivity and to open up access to new markets. This relationship is seldom a simple one. For example, a study by Röller and Waverman (2001) concluded that communications infrastructure development and economic growth can catalyse each other and that investment in telecommunications infrastructure has strong growth effects. However, it is acknowledged that these effects can be expected to kick in at a particular base level of universal access. In their article, Röller and Waverman point out that with penetration levels above 40 per cent there are significant growth effects. Their finding, however, is based only on fixed-line access and its associated infrastructure development (e.g. roads, electricity). Because South Africa has a relatively low fixed-line penetration rate, the potential growth effects the authors identify may well be limited.

For private access, telecommunications companies usually focus on areas where the general infrastructure is better, thereby avoiding poor rural areas. Nonetheless, the fact that cellphones are helping to bridge the telephonic divide between rich and poor is a positive development. Because cellphone towers are cheaper than traditional wires, these have been installed throughout the country, giving South Africa a coverage rate of more than 94 per cent.

Personal computer ownership will not grow, especially in remote rural areas, as long as purchase and service costs remain high. As noted, this is especially evident in the very poor rural areas, where residents are still deprived from up-to-date information and interaction with the world at large. Only around 13.6 per cent of households in South Africa has access to a computer, which is still crucial for Internet access for the majority of the country's population. Furthermore, only around 5.3 per cent of households in South Africa had access to the Internet in 2003. The impact of broadband or high-speed Internet access has been felt more strongly among existing users migrating from dial-up usage rather than in new users coming online. Disadvantaged communities have thus not benefited from broadband. It is also unlikely that residential broadband uptake will increase unless widespread connectivity at household level is made possible through lower installation costs and monthly charges.

Conclusions and recommendations

Public information and communication technology service centres definitely have a role to play in bridging the digital divide. The South African government has shown a commitment to redressing the imbalances of the past as far as ICT access is concerned. Tens of thousands of individuals across the country can potentially benefit from these centres. What is needed now is to establish how large the base of actual users is so that services can be provided optimally. However, at the same time, many municipalities still lag behind in terms of basic ICT provision to their communities.

Even though the various types of information and communication technology service centres have improved, communication possibilities for many people remain restricted. These disparities have an impact on the role that the information society is supposed to play as far as meeting the social and economic growth needs of the country.

Infrastructure development needs to address the backlog inherited from the previous government's preference for urban areas, because failure to do so will perpetuate the inequities of the past. At the same time, it must also be acknowledged that infrastructure is only part of the challenge – the other critical issue relates to the cost of access where infrastructure already exists.

In order to move towards an inclusive information society, South Africa needs meaningful data to identify disparities in access, to track progress and to make international comparisons. The collection of data without a clear structure is not particularly useful, so this activity needs to be informed by appropriate definitions of universal access and universal service. Part of this process should involve the regular evaluation of progress towards universal access. It is under these circumstances that policy-makers and the private sector can most effectively target the under-serviced areas of society.

7.2 Recommendations

To promote equitable distribution and access to ICT services, a number of recommendations are presented. The recommendations are grouped according to their focus on:
- ways of improving access to ICT, and improving research on ICT access; and
- supporting implementation of ICT infrastructure.

7.2.1 Information and research on ICT access

Access to data from the private sector
Generating a set of reliable ICT indicators through data collection requires collaboration between the role-players, and most notably from private sector service providers, to ensure that data are submitted on the basis of a shared agreement regarding the timing, format and comprehensiveness of submission. It is important to obtain such an undertaking so that progress in ICT penetration can be properly tracked. Service providers, government and citizens should have access to this kind of information. Recommendation: That the USAASA in collaboration with the Department of Communications and ICASA, formalise and benchmark the submission of relevant data so that ICT indicators can be developed.

Proritise data with the individual as unit of collection and analysis
Certain indicators in this publication were developed using survey data according to which the household was the unit of data collection and analysis. This was necessary

because data was not available from a census-type instrument. The standard approach to collecting data for the calculation of access indicators is based on per capita measures rather than per household measures. In developing countries, it may be useful to develop indicators based on both household and individual access.

Recommendation: That the USAASA in collaboration with the Department of Communications approach Statistics South Africa to obtain an arrangement regarding the collection of data that can be used in the creation of a sustainable set of ICT access indicators for South Africa. Further, that the relevant agencies measure ICTs in accordance with internationally accepted benchmarks, such as the Partnership for Measuring ICT 4D.

Mobilise multi-stakeholder partnerships in order to source data on ICT access
Infrastructure has been considered the main obstacle to improving access to ICTs. ICT access indicators are therefore often infrastructure-based, measuring such variables as the number of main telephone lines, and typically use the data of the telecommunication operators. But there is growing evidence to suggest that other factors, such as affordability and knowledge, are an important part of the access picture. Thus, the new environment requires access and usage indicators disaggregated according to socio-economic categories such as gender, income, age and location.

Recommendation: To measure the ICT picture in full, new multi-stakeholder partnerships are required. This should involve not only the statistical agencies such as Statistics South Africa, but also policy-makers, the private sector, civil society, non-governmental organisations and others involved in the ICT arena.

Understanding household ICT expenditure
Connectivity costs in South Africa have been a matter of public concern, with some attention being given to calculating international comparative costs for a standard service. However, insufficient attention has been given to analysing ICT costs from the perspective of the household. The emphasis here would be on the expenditure of households on a basket of ICT services and how households are able to balance the costs.

Recommendation: Investigate average household income in relation to a basket of telecommunication costs, and track household expenditure on telecommunications over time. This research will contribute to understanding ICT affordability.

Standardised ICT indicators
Individual and household data is required with a breakdown according to age, race, gender, occupation, income, etc. Furthermore, indicators are required to measure business access, as well as government access. Indicators are also required to determine social development, literacy, ICT skills, etc.

Recommendation: Standardised ICT indicators are required to measure individual, household, business, and government access. These indicators should be benchmarked against international indicators.

An integrated national ICT information framework
In order to prevent duplication and ad hoc research by various role-players, it is necessary to develop an integrated ICT information framework to coordinate various research activities.

Recommendation: National statistics and data gathering needs to be coordinated by putting an integrated information framework in place.

7.2.2. Implementation of ICT infrastructure

Speeding up the provision of ICT access by using available facilities such as libraries
It was observed that libraries as public facilities are logical places where ICT services could be made accessible. Libraries also have the widest spacial distribution of public ICT service centres measured in this research, therefore offering the widest potential impact. Increasingly, libraries are offering remote access to digital resources.

Recommendation: That the USAASA consider the possibility of working in partnership with provincial and municipal library services to expand the range of media available in the libraries to include computers with Internet capabilities, as well as peripherals such as printers and CD writers, so that people can access information.

Targeting of areas needing improvement in ICT penetration
The composite indicators reveal that there is a wide range in terms of available access to ICT across the more than 250 municipalities in South Africa. There is clearly a digital divide visible between municipalities that have much better access to ICT than others. The use of the composite indicators provides a comparative mechanism that takes into account conditions in all municipalities for planning purposes.

Recommendation: That the USAASA and other government agencies such as the Department of Provincial and Local Government consider working with municipalities that score low on the ICT indexes. This will require further interrogation of the data.

Monitor access to Community Service Telephones
Many remote areas, where population density is low and where the resident population is mainly low per-capita-income communities, have not adequately benefited from the CST initiative. Most CSTs are concentrated in areas with a high population density and with the least cost to service providers.

Recommendation: That the USAASA and other agencies monitor the current distribution of CSTs to ensure that the current pattern does not deteriorate. That ICASA specify the location of CST rollout where CST provision is part of future telecommunication providers licensing agreements. That existing licence holders' universal access objectives be re-evaluated in the light of the growth in the mobile phone industry and the continuing need for pro-poor ICT connectivity interventions.

Education and training provision
Implementing and maintaining ICT infrastructure and technology, especially in the rural areas, requires skilled people to service and maintain infrastructure and so to sustain ICT access.

Recommendation: Consider the rollout of education and training provision in areas where ICT infrastructure is to be rolled out.

Fair competition and affordable prices
Privatisation and liberalisation policies, together with regulatory capacity in the form of regulatory bodies, need to be put in place in order to assure fair competition among service providers and to assure affordable prices.

Recommendation: Restructuring of the market in South Africa to promote fair competition among service providers and to assure affordable delivery of ICT access.

APPENDICES

Appendix 1

Discussion of access to cellphones based on data from service providers

The data discussed in Chapter 2 was drawn from the HSRC's SASAS household survey (2003) and therefore reflects the telephone access conditions as reported by respondents. It is important to compare the data reported in Chapter 2 with the data provided by the cellphone service providers. This is an important exercise because it requires an understanding of how different kinds of data may provide quite a different picture of a particular situation. As will become clear below, the use of data for developing indicators of ICT access will have important consequences for the analysis.

A comparison of access to cellphones based on data obtained from service providers (Cell C, MTN, Vodacom) provides a different picture to that obtained from the household survey. The service providers provided counts of the number of users on their networks for 8 June 2005 between 05h00 and 10h00. The data were aggregated to fit the municipality boundaries. For the purpose of comparison, the data were expressed as the number of cellphones per 1 000 resident people. The number of cellphones per area as counted by the service providers were compared to counts of the resident population based on Census data. Cellphones were counted where they were being used, based on the position of the cellphone (actually its SIM card) as tracked/identified by each network provider. The position of the cellphone bore no relation to the home address of the user since the count was undertaken during the hours that people normally travel to work and begin their working day. The network providers did not supply the HSRC with any residential information about their clients, so the owner of the cellphone could not be traced to a household location. Moreover, since over 80 per cent of mobile subscribers are prepaid and not obliged to provide residential information, mapping cellphone owners to households would be nearly impossible. Currently, government is considering implementing regulations that require cellphone buyers to provide personal residential information.

When the data on cellphone user location was compared to data on the household residence of the population based on Census data, anomalies arose.

In the first instance, data were based on the physical count of technological devices (e.g. SIM cards as a proxy for mobile phone users) and not of individual users. Secondly, data were affected by the (obvious) fact that the devices were mobile and this would produce 'unusual' distributions of telephones as people moved around on the morning of the count. The fact that the count was undertaken in the morning can be expected to present a different pattern to if the count were taken at night, since most users would be at home. The problem here is that the devices could be switched off.

In Chapter 2, it was shown that the highest level of reported access to cellphones in any municipality did not exceed 70 per cent. Logic suggests that any one person should not need to use more than one mobile phone – with some exceptions, such as a worker keeping a personal cellphone in addition to a cellphone she/he may only use during working hours for calling only defined numbers. Based on these assumptions, the expectation was that there should not be more than one cellphone per person in any municipality. However, according to calculations based on data from the service providers, in which the number of cellphones counted on the morning in question was compared to the number of people resident in a municipality, there were 44 municipalities with more than 1 000 phones per 1 000 people at the time of the count. There are several reasons for this situation.

Firstly, some of the 44 municipalities have small resident populations but attract large numbers of visitors, such as in game or nature parks, places of historic interest, and other tourist-dense areas, as visible on the map in Figure 2.4. Other areas have small resident populations but they are situated near major transport arteries (e.g. the N1 through the Karoo) where many users pass through. Agricultural centres that do not have large residential populations also attract significant traffic, such as freight trucks, service vehicles, etc., which would most probably be equipped with tracking devices and/or cellphones.

In addition to the above conditions, individuals with multiple network connections (Cell C, Vodacom and MTN) were counted more than once, because each individual would have been counted as a customer by more than one of the service providers. Furthermore, telemetry devices might have inflated the count by service providers (i.e. SIM cards from the mobile networks that are used in vehicle tracking devices). Therefore, we can assume that the indicator as constructed from service-provider data were affected by the nature of the technology that was being tracked and the mobility of the population using the technology.

According to the data distribution shown on the histogram in Figure A, a large proportion of municipalities had between 100 to 400 users per 1 000 people.

Figure A: Distribution of cellphone users per 1 000 people by municipality

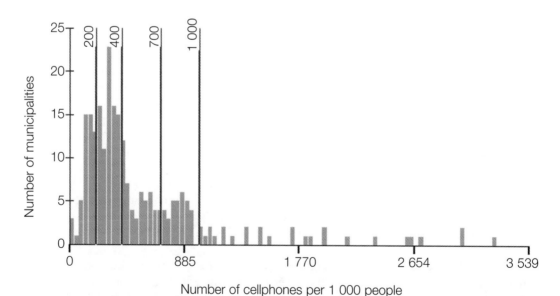

According to the service providers there were more than a 1 000 users per 1 000 people in the following municipalities (refer to Figure B):
- Laingsburg Municipality, Swartruggens, Langeberg Municipality, Kannaland Municipality, and Cedarberg Wilderness in the Western Cape;
- Kalahari Gemsbok Nature Reserve, Gordonia, Groblershoop, Namakwaland, Prieska and Tankwa-Karoo National Park in the Northern Cape;
- Baviaanskloof Widerness, Groendal Wilderness Area, Addo Elephant Nature Reserve, Cangos Kraal Nature Reserve, and Aberdeen in the Eastern Cape;
- Kimberley, Refengkgotso, Gariep Nature Reserve, and Tussen-die-Rivier Game Reserve in the Free State;
- Molopo Nature Reserve, Pilansberg Game Reserve, Marico Bosveld Nature Reserve, and Ventersdorp in the North West;
- The Kruger National Park, Musina, Lephalale, and Naboomspruit in Limpopo;
- The Kruger National Park, Thaba Chweu Municipality, Highlands Municipality, and Dipalaseng Municipality in Mpumalanga;
- Vereeniging and Mamelodi in Gauteng; and
- St Lucia, Mkuzi Game Reserve, Umfolozi Game Reserve, and the Kamberg Nature Reserve in KwaZulu-Natal.

The discussion has shown that calculating ratios of cellphones per 1 000 people on the basis of actual cellphone location will produce anomalous data, especially where populations are highly mobile and are required to commute on a daily basis for work reasons. It is possible that the data are more reliable in areas where the population is less mobile and is not working in occupations that require movement from the place of residence to the place of work.

In the following areas there were less than 200 cellphone users per 1 000 people:
- Kai! Garib Municipality and Khara Hais Municipality in the Northern Cape;
- Senqu, Matatiele, Umzimvubu, Elundini, Mbizana, Qaukeni, Mhlontlo, Sakhisizwe, Ematahleni, Intsika Yethu, Engcobo, and Nyandeni Municipalites in the Eastern Cape;
- Phuthaditjhaba (in the former QwaQwa homeland) in the Free State;
- Moshaweng, the Greater Taung, and Lekwa-Teemane Municipalities in North West;
- Mbibana magisterial district in the Mkobola area in Mpumalanga; and
- Umhlabuyalingana, eDumbe, Utrecht, Abaqulusi, Nongoma, and Msinga Municipalities in Kwa-ZuluNatal.

As can be seen from the observations made in the discussion, there are limits to the usefulness of analysing data from service providers for the construction of an indicator of access where the cellphone (or SIM-card data) is not linked to individual owners and their residence. Given that the majority of users obtained services by means of ad hoc pre-paid methods, there is by definition no means of establishing their place of residence. Data from service providers in the format provided do not suit the requirements of this indicator-based analysis.

Figure B: Cellphone users per 1 000 people

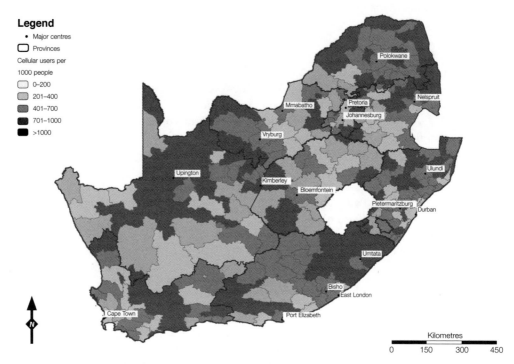

Source: Cell C, MTN, Vodacom 2005

It must be emphasised that on the figure above, the dark areas (>1000) are sparsely populated, but they also cover massive geographic extents. This potentially gives the incorrect impression that mobile coverage is quite good in rural areas, even with over-counting. However, that is a false impression. There is the possibility that a reader who is unaware of rural demographics could draw the incorrect conclusion that private or household cellphone access is not a problem in rural areas.

Appendix 2

Indicators

Indicator Number	Indicator description
1	Access to telephone landlines
2	Access to cellphones
3	Access to Community Service Telephones
4	Access to computers
5	Access to the Internet
6	Access to Multi-Purpose Community Centres (MPCCs)
7	Access to telecentres
8	Access to Cyberlabs
9	Access to Public Information Terminals (PITs)
10	Access to libraries
11	Location and operation of Under-Serviced Area Licenses
12	Composite indicator 1 (Private access)
13	Composite indicator 2 (Public access)

Appendix 3

Relevant South African Policy and Legislation

Republic of South Africa (1995): Green Paper on Telecommunications Policy

Republic of South Africa (1996): Telecommunications Act

Republic of South Africa (1996): White Paper on Telecommunications (Second Draft)

Republic of South Africa (1996): White Paper on Telecommunications

Republic of South Africa (1996–2001): Consolidated Telecommunications Act

Republic of South Africa (2000): Independent Communications Authority of South Africa Act

Republic of South Africa (2001): Telecommunications Amendment Act

Republic of South Africa (2002): Electronic Communications and Transactions Act

Republic of South Africa (2002): Regulation of Interception of Communications and Provision of Communication-related Information Act

Republic of South Africa (2004): Draft Convergence Bill

REFERENCES

Benjamin, P. (2002) Reviewing Universal Access in South Africa, in *The Southern African Journal of Information and Communication* 2(1). http://link.wits.ac.za/journal/j0201-pb.htm

Benjamin, P. (2003) *The Universal Service and Access Agency of South Africa's telecentre programme: 1998–2000*. Cape Town: HSRC Publishers

Burrows, T. (2005) Vodacom, MTN neck and neck, in *iWeek*, 14, 4 August 2005

Butcher, N. (1998) *The possibilities and pitfalls of harnessing ICTs to accelerate social development: A South African perspective*. The South African Institute for Distance Education, http://www.saide.org.za/butcher1/unrisd.htm

CITI (Cape Information Technology Initiative) & WESGRO (Western Cape Investment and Trade Promotion Agency) (2001), http://www.strategis.ic.gc.ca/epic/internet/inimrri.nsf/fr/gr105443f.html

Canada High Commission Trade Office (2005) *ICT in South Africa*, http://www.canadasachamber.com/news/index.cfm?fuseaction=NewsDetail&newsid=76

Castells, M. (2000) Information Technology and Global Development. Keynote address at the Economic and Social Council of the United Nations, New York, 12 May 2000

Conradie, D.P., Morris, C. & Jacobs, S.J. (2003) Using Information and Communication Technologies (ICTs) for deep rural development in South Africa, in *Communication*, 29 (1&2), 199–217

Economist Intelligence Unit (2005) *South Africa: Telecoms and Technology background*, http://www.ebusinessforum.com/index.asp?layout=newdebi&country_id=ZA&chan

Esselaar, S. & Stork, C. (2005) Mobile cellular telephone: Fixed-line substitution in Sub-Saharan Africa, in *The Southern African Journal of Information and Communication*, forthcoming

Gillwald, A. (2005) *Towards an African e-Index Access and Usage*. Johannesburg: LINK Centre, University of the Witwatersrand

Gillwald, A., Esselaar, S., Burton, P., & Stavrou, A. (2004) *Towards an e-Index for South Africa: Measuring household and individual access and usage of ICT*. Johannesburg: LINK Centre, University of the Witwatersrand

Gillwald, A., Esselaar, S., Burton, P., & Stavrou, A. (2005) South Africa, in Gillwald, A. (ed) *Towards an African e-Index: Household and individual ICT access and usage across 10 African countries*. Johannesburg: LINK Centre, University of the Witwatersrand

Global Insight (2004) *Global Insight Southern Africa*, Centurion: Global Insight Southern Africa, http://www.globalinsight.com

Goldstuck, A. (2005) *Internet Access in South Africa*, http://www.theworx.biz/access05.htm

Gómez, R., & Hunt, P. Lamoureaux (1999) *Telecentre evaluation: A global perspective*. Report of an international meeting on telecentre evaluation, Far Hills Inn, Quebec, Canada, 28–30 September

GCIS (Government Communications and Information Service) (2001) *Multi-purpose Community Centre*, http://www.gcis.gov.za

Guislain, P., Ampah, M.A., Besançon, L., Niang, C. & Sérot, A. (2005) *Connecting Sub-Saharan Africa*, Washington: The World Bank

Hendry, J.D. (2000) Social inclusion and the information poor, in *Library Review* 49 (7)1–8

Horwitz, R.B. (1997) Telecommunications policy in the new South Africa: Participatory politics and sectoral reform, in *Communication* 23 (2): 63–78

Hodge, J. (2004) Universal service through roll-out targets and licence conditions: Lessons from telecommunications in South Africa, in *Development Southern Africa* 21(1), 205–225

HSRC (2003) *South African Social Attitude Survey 2003*. HSRC: Pretoria

ICT World (2005) USAL licence areas cover roughly 45% of the population BMI-T, in *ICT World Editorial* 124, 7–14 February 2005

Jacobs, S.J. & Herselman, E. (2005) An ICT-Hub model for rural communities, in *International Journal of Education and Development using Information and Communication Technology (IJEDICT)*, 1(3): 57–93

Knott-Craig, A. (2005) SA cellphones pass two affordability tests, in *Business Report* 03/08/2005, http://www.busrep.co.za/general/ArticleId-2814994, accessed 15 October 2005

Levin, A. (2005) Internet society (South Africa) *Internet Fiesta*, http://www.ispa.org.za/iweek/2005.presentation.shtm

Mansell, R. & Wehn, U. (eds) (1998) *Knowledge societies: Information technology for sustainable development*. Oxford University Press

Oyedemi, T. (2005) Universal access wheel: Towards achieving universal access to ICT in Africa, in *Southern African Journal of Information and Communication* (5) 90–107

Oestmann, S., & Dymond, C.A. (2001) Telecentres – Experiences, Lessons and Trends, in Latchem & Walker (eds) *Telecentres: Case studies and Key issues*, Commonwealth of Learning

Pillay, K. (1998) Discussion paper on Definition of Universal Service and Universal Access in South Africa, in *Government Gazette*, Vol. 400, 19397

Quantec Research (2003–2004) *Quantec database*, Menlo Park: Quantec Research (Pty) Ltd., http://www.quantec.co.za

Röller, L., & Waverman, L. (2001) *Telecommunications Infrastructure and Economic Development: A Simultaneous approach, discussion paper no. 2399*, London Centre for Economic Policy Research, http://www.shef.ac.uk/uni/academic/N-Q/perc/ripe/Ed.Stat.html

Sithole, P. (2004) *Universal service and access in the telecommunications industry*. Research report for the National Labour and Economic Development Institute, April 2004

Standard Bank, MWEB Business & Microsoft (2005) *SMMEs have what it takes to hold their own: Findings from SME Survey*, http://www.theworx.biz/sme05c.htm

Statistics South Africa (2001) *Census 2001 Key Results*, http://www.statssa.gov.za

USAASA (Universal Service and Access Agency of South Africa) (2004) *Promoting universal access to ICT services in South Africa: Background*, http://www.usa.org.za/ginfo.html

USAASA (2005) Unpublished data made available to the HSRC

Warschauer, M. (2003) *Technology and Social Inclusion: Rethinking the Digital Divide*. Cambridge: MIT Press

WorldWatch Institute (2004) *More Mobile & Telecoms Stats*, http://www.cellular.co.za/news_2004/Jan/030304-cell phones_bridge_global_difital.htm

World Wild Worx (2005) *The Impact of Mobile Technology on Corporate South Africa*, http://www.theworx.biz/mobile05b.htm

World Wide Worx, Cell C & First National Bank (2005) *Mobility 2005 Project*, http://www.theworx.biz/mobile05b.htm

World Wild Worx, Razor's Edge Business Intelligence & Trigrammic (2005) *Map of the IT and Telecoms Sector (MITTS)*, http://www.theworx.biz/mitts05.htm

Zaaiman, B. (2004) *Softstart probes size, shape of ICT small businesses in Gauteng.* ITWeb, http://www.itweb.co.za/sections/business/2004/0408050825.asp?A=SME&S=SME&O=FPIN